PARISH PRIEST

PARISH
PRIEST

FATHER LeROY E. McWILLIAMS

WITH Jim Bishop

McGraw-Hill Book Company, Inc.
New York Toronto London

PARISH PRIEST

Nihil obstat:
JOHN M. A. FEARNS, S.T.D., *Censor Librorum*

Imprimatur:
✠ FRANCIS CARDINAL SPELLMAN, *Archbishop of New York*

New York: February 9, 1953

*The nihil obstat and imprimatur are official declara-
tions that a book or pamphlet is free of doctrinal or
moral error. No implication is contained therein that
those who have granted the nihil obstat and imprimatur
agree with the contents, opinions, or statements expressed.*

Published by the McGraw-Hill Book Company, Inc.
Printed in the United States of America

In loving memory of
my father and mother
James and Henrietta McWilliams

1

Someday, when my time comes, the undertaker may be surprised to find, if he looks closely, a small smile on the face of the deceased. If so, it will be a smile of gratitude because God has been so very good—so extra-specially good—to me in so many ways, and the smile will also be there because my father and my mother left to me a legacy of laughter, the humor to see how ridiculous and small I am, and the opportunity to see other men and events in the same light.

In the time allotted to me, I have learned that man is a grim animal, and the grimmer he gets the more he amuses me. At the exact moment of his birth, he is punished by a doctor's hand, and he cries. To my way of thinking, he cries from that point onward, in one way or another. He climbs upward, slowly and painfully, on a hill of slippery sand. No matter how high he goes, he wants to go higher; and, if he attains the top, he stares downward in fear of his friends, who are climbing right behind him. He is never completely satisfied; seldom completely happy. He fights at the moment of death just as he fought at the moment of life—he doesn't want to go, just as he never wanted to be born.

Me, I'm a priest. A small priest among scores of thousands of priests. In my heart I know I'm not so fine a priest as many others I have known. And my road has not been so difficult as that of—well, the missionaries, who struggle against language barriers and ancient heathen creeds and a quiet brand of hate which can boil up into sudden death at any moment. No, my life of service cannot compare with theirs.

Why then, you ask, is a book being written about my life?

I'm Irish, or rather of Irish descent. I have spent more than a quarter of a century in one parish, St. Michael's in Jersey City. It's an old-fashioned Irish-Polish-Italian parish, small in size geographically, but large in the number of its parishioners and large at heart. The story I have to tell is more of St. Michael's than of myself. It is good for a man's soul to take a complete inventory of his life—a broad examination of conscience, as it were—and I'm going to try it.

Across the Hudson River from New York is a big, grimy town called Jersey City. That's where I live. It attained its greatest glory in the 1890s, when the Irish immigrants were being let off the boat by the thousands. Many of them settled in a downtown area about a mile square. Part of that area, in St. Michael's Parish, is called Cork Row. These Irish were not rich, lace-curtain Irish. They were big men with rich brogues who had hands like hams and who worked in the sugar refinery, or down at the docks, or in an oil refinery in Greenville. They worked hard and they drank hard, and they all married angels who had the tolerance and the temperament to keep them on God's holy path. They had tremendous families, and it was always a problem keeping little Timothy in shoes, or trying to keep the back of his pants intact.

It was a parish of flats—cold-water tenements, if you please—jammed tight one against another, with mothers always leaning out the window on the fourth or fifth floor, yelling down to Patricia not to forget to get a loaf of bread and to tell Mr. Schultz that Daddy would give him the money on payday. It was that kind of parish. It was a place of street brawls and love, of broken skulls and broken hearts; a place where a boy who couldn't lick his way through the third grade had better not come back for the fourth; a place where a man might boast of any crime in the book except that of missing Mass; a place where the poor took up collections to pay the rent of someone less fortunate; a parish of marriages and births and deaths; a place where the freckle-faced tough kid who assists at Mass today might indeed become the gentle priest of tomorrow.

I wouldn't trade St. Michael's for a cathedral.

And yet, the parish has slipped a bit since those grand days. A city, like a person, grows outward. The nub of Jersey City, in the old days, was in Cork Row, or the Horseshoe, as it was called. But as the children grew to adulthood, the Horseshoe wasn't good enough for them. In truth, many of them were a little ashamed of the old neighborhood. So they moved outward, away from St. Michael's. They moved to the sections which were then considered "classy"—the Bergen section, Greenville, the Heights.

The old-timers stayed on, and many of them are still in the Horseshoe. That's why, perhaps, before any Mass at St. Michael's, you will see many men with snowy hair, many women grasping pew after pew as they work their way up toward the front of the church. We see more old people than usual because they have refused to be transplanted elsewhere.

Then too, when the Holland Tunnel came, the approaches cut through a strong part of St. Michael's parish, and whole blocks of tenements were razed to make way for the tile gullet. Some of the old flats have been condemned, and the buildings stand empty, staring at the passers-by through the blindness of broken windows and dark interiors.

Still, St. Michael's is far from being a dying parish. It has a vigor unmatched, I believe, anywhere else. There are more Communion breakfasts in the basement of our church than anywhere else. Not long ago, I watched almost the entire department of the Hudson County police force walk up the center aisle in full uniform to receive Communion at the rail. This may not sound extraordinary to you, but you should have seen those loaded guns swinging from the hips. And when those men, after Mass, went down to the basement of the church, they piled into platters of ham steaks and eggs and rolls, and had a wonderful time. When I told the jokes, they smiled politely. When Jackie Gleason, the television star, told the jokes, they practically rolled under the tables. It was obvious to me, at that moment, that I did not miss my vocation.

We have a beautiful church, a big convent, an elementary school, a high school, and, diagonally across the street from the church, St. Francis Hospital. The hospital does not belong to the church, but I cite these things to show you that it is a very Catholic neighborhood. In front of the hospital and around it are signs that proclaim, QUIET—HOSPITAL and NO TRUCKING. One day a truck ran through Hamilton Place, in front of the hospital, and a policeman stopped the truck.

It was a warm, rich afternoon, and I paced up and down on the sidewalk reading my breviary. The cop put one foot on the running board of the truck and let loose a blast of

4

blasphemy that would peel the paint off the hood. A woman walked up to me horror-stricken.

"Father," she said, "do ya hear that now? Isn't it awful?"

I looked her squarely in the eye and said, "Lady, that's police language. You and I can't understand a word of it."

Still, when I think of St. Michael's, of the wonders and the terrors of the parish, a special recollection always comes to mind. I think of the black, rainy night that a phone call came to the rectory. I heard the ringing and turned on the light next to my bed. The voice on the phone was heavy with whisky.

"Father, can you come right down? I'm at Sweeney's Bar. A man was standing at the bar drinking, and he suddenly caved in, Father. He's laying in the sawdust, and if he passes out without the last rites. . . ."

"Who is he?" I said.

"I don't properly know his name, Father. But he lives in the neighborhood. I've seen him at Sweeney's."

A priest has no right to meditate on the worthiness of a dying man. Yet, I thought twice before walking into a drunken setting with the Sacred Host on my person. I got up, got dressed as quickly as possible, and went to Sweeney's determined to render conditional Absolution to the unconscious man.

And yet, the moment I entered I began to wonder whether I was right or wrong. The place smelled of stale beer and whisky. But on the bar, directly over the victim, were a crucifix and two lighted candles. Every drunk in the place had moved away from the bar, and, the moment I entered, all hats were removed, and every man dropped to his knees.

It taught me that the true love and fear of God are not al-

5

ways found in church. Those men, some of them besotted with drink, felt that I carried God on my person, and they knew instinctively what to do in His presence.

When I think of St. Michael's, I think of that.

Still, it isn't a big parish. I heard of one in the Carolinas which measures 125 square miles. St. Michael's is seven blocks in one direction and eight in the other, but in that small area are 1000 Catholic families jammed shoulder to shoulder. It is not uncommon to find ten families in a tenement flat who are parishioners of St. Michael's.

Probably the single most important duty of a priest is to maintain contact with these people—all of them. The pastor must know the true state, spiritual and temporal, of his parishioners. Their troubles are his troubles; their losses are his losses; their small happinesses are reflected in his eyes. To be blunt, it was no problem for me to keep close contact with my parishioners because, in the first place, I love people—all kinds of people—and, in the second place, I am naturally inquisitive. It would have been a problem to keep me apart from my flock.

In St. Michael's, there is less than a handful of persons, men, women, or children, whom I do not know by name and whose domestic life I cannot trace at will. The greatest contacts, of course, between priest and parishioners are the pulpit, the confessional, and the altar. In these he leads their spiritual welfare, he points the way. In the confessional, in the name of Jesus Christ, he counsels, advises, forgives, and punishes. Here he sees the bared soul, the weaknesses and the excuses; he listens, with eyes averted, to the prattling "sins" of the little girl who fibbed, not once, but twice, in the past week, and he also, on occasion, hears the changing voice of the adolescent who stole from the candy store when the proprietor wasn't looking. He knows that none of them are hopeless, or else they wouldn't be in the confessional, in shame and sorrow, ready to throw themselves on the mercy of God.

I cannot break the seal of the confessional to relate any specific matters, but I can tell you of one occasion when a woman came into the box to seek aid, not to confess. It happened on a Saturday afternoon, and a long line of children extended down the aisle of the dimly lit church. The woman came in and asked for help. I asked her if she was prepared for confession, and she said no, that she was very much upset and had to see me at once. That's why she had stood in the confessional line. I asked her what the trouble was, and she told me that her daughter, a student in St. Michael's High School, was going to become a mother. It is on these occasions that the heart bleeds.

I told the lady that I must continue to hear confessions, that the confessional was not the place for the discussion she ached for, and that she could see me at the rectory any morning of the week. She arrived on Sunday morning shortly after eight. Physically, she was amazing. She was one of the tallest women I've ever seen, and her blond hair was tied in two big braids behind her neck. Her face was creased with pain. She sat and she told me that her daughter had had an argument with her about staying out late, and the daughter had packed a bag and walked out of the house. She ended up in Newark, New Jersey, walking the streets. A man followed her; the child became frightened. She saw a middle-aged man walking toward her, and she entreated him to walk with her to keep the other man from following. They walked together for a while, the man quieting her fears, and then he walked her into a house, locked the door, and assaulted the child. Thus the pregnancy.

I didn't believe it either.

7

However, my job was not to reason whether the story was credible or not; my function was to acknowledge that a young girl in my high school was in trouble—deep trouble —and that I had been asked to do something about it. The mother wondered if I wanted to interview her daughter. I said no, that such a course would only deepen the shame of the girl, and that the mother could answer any questions I might ask. Soon after she left, thanking me for things I had not done, I got busy. The first thing I did was to phone a hospital far out of town and arrange with the medical superintendent for the admission of the girl ahead of time. This was so that she would not become the butt of bitter gibes in the neighborhood, as her condition became pronounced. The next thing was to ask, through the mother, whether the girl wanted to keep the baby. The answer was no. The third thing was to get a friendly local doctor to write a note to the girl's teacher, saying that the girl had a mysterious ailment which had been tentatively identified as a perforated ulcer, and that she would have to be hospitalized for three months. It was suggested that she could keep up with her studies while in the sickbed.

All of this was done. The girl went to the hospital and had her baby, a fine boy with tight-shut eyes, curling fists, and black hair plastered all over his head. The girl kept up with her studies. She had no trouble with other patients because she was registered under an assumed name. It seems almost like the hand of God to me that, four days after the baby was born, a wealthy woman from New York, a patron of the hospital, was walking through the infants' ward with a sister of charity when she paused at the crib of the little one that nobody wanted. She looked down and smiled.

"What a baby!" she said. "You know, Sister, my husband and I have been married eighteen years, and we've prayed

8

and prayed and prayed, but no baby ever came to us. If we ever have one, I'd want it to be like this one."

The sister smiled. "That one," she said softly, "is up for adoption."

The rich lady adopted the little boy. The girl student returned to our high school in time to don cap and gown and graduate with her class. No one ever knew. The baby boy is now growing up with the finest advantages in the world, and will soon be eligible for army service. The girl has long since married, has other children of her own, and is very happy.

Not all these personal contacts with the people end so happily. Many years ago, we had a young policeman in the parish—we had several, but I speak of Johnny because I could never look at him without admiration—and he had everything a young man should have. He was as big as a bungalow, and he spoke in polite whispers. He was as handsome as a man would dare be. He was liked by his lieutenants and captains, and he was on the way up in the police department. He was devoted to his old Irish mother and father and bought a car for them so that he could take them around the countryside on his days off. He had a fiancée who can best be described as a jewel. She was pretty and she was modest, and she loved Johnny and she worshiped his parents, as they did her, and the date was set.

One day Johnny and his girl attended a nuptial Mass for two close friends, and they attended the wedding breakfast and the merrymaking afterward. At the breakfast Johnny ate with his left hand and Alice ate with her right, because the other two hands were clasped together under the table. They whispered frequently, and I guess that they saw in this their own wedding feast soon to come. That night Johnny went on duty, a block from St. Michael's. The night was

9

clear and warm, and the hours after midnight were silent.

In the morning Johnny had not reported off duty. Two men from the bureau of patrol went out looking for him, and they found him. He was dead in the back of a parked car. He was half slumped on the floor, and one arm reached for the far side of the car and didn't quite make it. Johnny the handsome, Johnny the happy, had died of a heart attack during the night. I was called immediately. It is impossible for me to explain the shock I felt. I was speechless. Perhaps "stunned" is a better word. A priest gets accustomed to the presence of death, but it was beyond my belief that the gigantic, happy, healthy boy of yesterday was this crumpled, dusty uniform before me. I administered conditional Absolution, although, knowing how Johnny lived, I had little worry that he was prepared to stand before the throne of God and give a good accounting of his life.

The police reasoned, from the dust on the front of the uniform, that when he first sustained the attack, Johnny had probably cried out for help and the cry echoed up and down the empty streets and that, unable to stand, he had fallen and crept, on his belly, to a parked car and crawled inside to die.

The cops—always generous—said that they would break the news to Johnny's fiancée if I would do as much for his mother and father. It was a formidable task, made almost impossible by the effusive greeting I got when I walked into their little flat. Please believe me when I tell you that there is no easy way. One of the first things the proud mother said was, "Now, Johnny will be home soon and I'm fixing coffee and buns for him, and you might as well sit down."

The lump in my throat got bigger and bigger until I couldn't talk at all. I sat staring at the faded rug in the dining room until the parents began to look at each other and then at me. Then I blurted it out. I said it quickly, softly, compassionately, aching in every fiber as the words tumbled. No story, no picture, can ever convey that scene, and I pray to God that I will never have to witness one, or be a part of one, again. The wailing, the lamentation, of mother and father, the screams that brought the neighbors running, the father pounding the walls with his fists as the tears staggered down his cheeks—never, never will I forget.

Now and then there was a letup of the mother's grief, as though reason had returned and she knew that Johnny could not be dead.

"That lily there on the window," she murmured, tearing at her cheek with her hand, "he bought it for me for Easter." And then, with obvious pride, "And the box of candy, too. He never bought a box of candy for Alice that he didn't buy one for me. He said for us not to fret over him getting married, that he'd take care of Pop and me. Oh, but he was such a good boy. Every morning he brought up the wood and the coal, and he couldn't be thinking of enough things to make us happy." Then she looked tired, and she said, "Will somebody shut off the coffee?" And somebody did.

As a priest, I was a total failure. I could not console, because I wasn't consoled myself. My heart was like a rock. I told the old lady that Johnny had received Communion only two days before, that he wouldn't appear empty-handed, but my words served only to force her mind to understand that Johnny was indeed dead, irrevocably dead, and that she would not see him again in this life.

Now and then, when someone is helped by a priest, the entire matter turns out so well that even the cleric is gratified. We had a man—I'll call him Tom Smith—who was arrested out in the Middle West for stealing a car. The record showed that he hadn't been a very good boy when he was at St. Michael's. I didn't know that car theft could be a Federal offense, but in Tom's case it was, and he drew three years. When he had served two, his sister came to the rectory and said that the parole board would shorten his sentence if I would be his parolee. I had some misgivings about it, but then I thought that if I didn't help, and Tom was really sincere this time, my lack of action might embitter him to the point of helping him to return to crime. So I said yes, I'd help. The sister was thankful, and she pointed out that one of the conditions of parole was that Tom would have to be guaranteed a job before he left prison, and he would have to start working within twenty-four hours after his arrival home or be subject to immediate return to prison. Well, before I signed the application, I went out all over the parish in stores and shops and industrial companies, trying to get Tom a job. In no case did I lie or evade. I explained the case and said that I was sure that Tom would be a good boy in the future. At long last I found an employer who was willing to take a chance, and the application was dispatched to the West. The sister and I waited, but nothing happened. It was months later before Tom was released, and by that time the waiting job had been filled.

One afternoon Tom walked into the rectory, a rather tall young man, dark of hair and eyes, and pleasant-looking. We chatted awhile, and I began to think, from his attitude, that he might be a good risk. He didn't try to excuse his crime, but he pointed out that the Federal record showed that two men had offered him a lift to California if he would assume the duty of driver. That's how he was caught with a stolen car. I found out another thing: he no longer lived in St. Michael's, and I had been breaking my back trying to find a position for him. It was too late to back out now, and he kept reminding me that he had to have a job by morning. I took him out with me, and we traipsed the streets together, from one place to another. And—I got Tom a job. I almost bludgeoned the owner of a taxicab to hire the boy, but hired he was, and he went to work in the morning. Thereafter, every month for three years Tom had to report to the rectory to tell me what he was doing, how much he had saved, whether he had got into any trouble, and so forth. And each month I dutifully filled out the Federal questionnaire and filed it with the parole office in Newark. Those three years have long since been ticked off in sunsets, and Tom is now a most law abiding citizen and has enough money put away for several rainy days.

No one ever comes to see me to bring good news. To my knowledge, no one ever rang the doorbell to announce that "the whole family is working, my husband is on the wagon, the children have been getting nothing but the highest marks in school, the rent is paid six months in advance, we all received Communion together last Sunday, and so much money is coming in that I've had to stuff some of it in the mattress." No, that never happened. And I don't think I'll live long enough to see it happen. And, if it did happen, it might have the effect of finishing me off right then and there.

In St. Michael's, the priest is the court of last resort. It has always been this way, and I wouldn't want it changed. The welfare of my people is a large part of my duties. Few of our Michaelians ever resort to a court of law. Divorce is so rare that, when it occurs, it is a conversational tidbit for months. Theft by juveniles more often comes to me for adjudication than to the police. Husbands who look upon the grape with too much devotion become my penitents. Wives who nag have sat in my office by the scores. So have daughters who know more than their mothers. And so have sons who are shiftless and supremely certain that the world owes them a living.

We've had a few families in the parish who have been getting money from the rectory weekly for thirty years. These are the shiftless ones. They aren't many, but they are less than adolescent mentally, and they want no work and no responsibility. Conversely, these breed the largest families, do less for their children than others, and expect the most when the children grow up. In most of these cases, I know that I'm a prime sucker, but I do not dare to stop the weekly payments because to do so would hurt innocent children.

When they need the priest, they'll find him no matter where he is. Last summer, a woman tracked me to a lake where I have a cabin. She wasn't at all abashed. If anything, she seemed slightly resentful that I was not at the rectory when she wanted me. I asked her what the trouble was, and she said that her husband was in jail again—six months, this time—and that she had no rent money and that the landlord was threatening to pitch her and her brood out on the street. Would I help? I told her to go to the Mount Carmel Guild, on Bay Street, to tell them that I had sent her, and to ask for a month's rent. She got it. She never phoned a thank-you, but I'll be hearing from her again, I know.

It has been my pride that I know not only my own flock but also nearly everyone else within the geographical confines of St. Michael's—Protestant, Jew, atheist, and nonpracticing Catholic—but now and then I get fooled. One warm evening at dusk, I walked to the back window of the rectory for a breath of air. Below me was a high wall, which divides church from rectory and church from high-school annex. Two boys were standing on it, one about nine, one about eleven. The nine-year-old was urinating on the wall. I looked at them, but couldn't recall having seen them before. While I was looking, the older boy jumped down off the wall and ran toward our gymnasium.

14

Matters had gone far enough. I left the window, hurried downstairs and out the door, and, in a long cassock which will always keep a priest from doing 100 yards in less than 15 seconds, I ran around the block just as the older boy was trying to climb the wall again.

"Say," I said, "this is private property, boys. Get off that wall and stay off."

The little one looked down at me. His mouth curled with disgust. "Why, you dirty bum! You dirty bum, you!" he yelled. The older boy, at that point, broke and ran. I chased him down the block, but God had blessed his feet with the wings of Mercury and I turned back just in time to find the younger one running pell-mell behind me. I grabbed him, pinned his arms to his side, and shook him until his teeth rattled. I warned him never to use those words again. When he left, he was crying, rubbing his eyes with grimy hands, and running—all at the same time.

When I returned to the rectory, I was still mystified about the identity of the boys, and somewhat chagrined, because it had now been proved that I didn't know everybody in St. Michael's. I was barely in my office when the phone rang. A woman spoke.

"Are you the priest that just beat up a little boy on Tenth Street?"

"Who is this, please?"

"Never mind that. Are you the one that beat up the little boy, is what I want to know. He's got lacerations, and I'm going to swear out a warrant for your arrest."

"If he has lacerations, madam, I didn't put them there. In any case, I think the warrant is a good idea. You do that."

Suddenly, she roared, "Why, you dirty bum, you!" and, from that slight clew, I gathered that this was the fine mother of the fine boys. I found out later that the family had moved into St. Michael's that very week, so I no longer felt badly about not recognizing the boys.

I prided myself on knowing not only the people in my section, but those in other sections as well. This is especially true of the downtown area of Jersey City. For instance, although the Catholic religion is, by its very nature, clannish, three of the men for whom I had the utmost respect were Protestant ministers. Canon Bryan is one. He's dead now, but he worked as hard as anyone in the Lord's vineyard. He was pastor of Grace Episcopal Church on Second Street, and I think that every priest who met him liked him at once. He was a broad-shouldered man, quiet, circumspect, always busy tending to his small flock, and not a bit envious of giant St. Mary's R.C. Church across the street. He had a tolerance for other faiths that could well be imitated and practiced by others, including some Catholics. When Catholic friends of the canon died, he attended the Requiem Mass. I have heard bigots talk against every faith and every clergyman by name, but I have never heard anyone say a word against Canon Bryan. One bigot inadvertently bestowed upon the canon the highest of all praise when he muttered, "Well, he's different."

There were others. Pastor Edward Grubb, a Lutheran minister, is the Protestant chaplain of the Jersey City Fire Department. His great gift is that he loves all people—whole blocks of them at a time—and he cares not what their faith may be. There are more Catholics than Protestants in the fire department, but the Catholics vie for Pastor Grubb's smile as much as those of other creeds. There are others— many of them. Pastor Emeritus Alfred Sadler of the Claremont Presbyterian Church is one. Today, in partial retirement, Pastor Sadler collects old Bibles. As a preacher he was the very embodiment of true tolerance and of true scholarship.

One day we got a call, a real rush call, from Henderson Street, and a priest galloped over at high speed. When he got inside the door of the flat, the trouble was obvious. The lady of the house, without a stitch of clothing, was running back and forth through the rooms screaming at the top of her lungs and brandishing a knife. Her husband, who was scared to death and made no attempt to get near her, said that she wasn't intoxicated. The priest didn't know what to do, and I guess he wondered why he had been called in the first place. She came racing back from the parlor toward him, and when she saw the Roman collar she stopped, stared, and dropped the knife. Quickly, he ran to a closet, grabbed a heavy winter coat, and threw it to her. She put it on, and then she burst into tears. The priest walked toward her, slowly, not menacing in any way, and talked quietly and compassionately and told her that she was all upset and needed a rest. He asked her if she didn't think it would be best to go to a hospital where she could get the best of care. She looked up at him, her eyes brimming with tears, and nodded dumbly. That closed the incident. The poor lady was —in the parlance of the times—off her rocker.

I don't know why they call a priest in situations like this, but they do. Two cripples, an old man and his wife, phoned to ask me to save them from being dispossessed. They lived several miles outside my parish, and my calling has nothing to do with rent control, but I was elected to help. And I did. I drove to the Federal Housing Authority, got the file on the case, and told the director that there was nothing in there to make plain that the parties involved were, in fact, hopeless cripples and that both lived in wheel chairs. With the help

17

of Catholic Charities, I got a check for several months' rent and had the man and his wife back in their apartment by nightfall.

Matters can be rough enough within the confines of St. Michael's without going outside to look for more trouble. But still the calls come, and though the priest vows that he'll never stir outside his own parish again, he does it "just once more." A young lady came to the rectory, some years ago, wringing her hands. I asked what the trouble was, and she said that her father was dying in North Hudson Hospital, and would I go to see him right away. The father didn't come from St. Michael's, and besides, he was Protestant although the rest of the family was Catholic. There must be a tactful way of saying no, but I haven't learned it yet. I told her that I'd visit her father at once, but that I didn't know what good I could do, or even whether I'd be welcome at a time like that. When I got to the hospital, I found that Captain John Tell, formerly of the Hudson River Day Line, was indeed on the way out. He was so big that he must have been just short of seven feet tall. His feet hung out a foot through the bars at the bottom of the bed. He was lucid, and spoke in whispers. Nobody was fooling the captain—he knew that the curtain was falling. He lay there, looking at me with a great, mute longing in his eyes. We talked for a while, and I tried to cheer him up. We didn't discuss death. We talked about sickness and pain and convalescence. When I got ready to go and took my hat off the clothes tree in the room, he seemed on the verge of asking me to stay. It was obvious that he wanted me with him.

I told him that I'd pray for his recovery, and, as I turned the knob of the door, I said casually, over my shoulder, "Have you ever thought of becoming Catholic, like your wife and children?"

The voice, which once boomed to deck hands, whispered hoarsely, "Nobody ever asked me."

I dropped the hat and asked him if he realized what he was saying. He nodded. I asked him if he would like me to convert him now. (At best he had a couple of hours left.) He smiled, for the first time, and said yes. I took off out of that room and down the slippery corridor and found a nurse and got a pitcher and a basin and some water, and I skidded back into the room and baptized the captain absolutely and then administered to him the last rites of the Church.

Later, he asked, "Am I a Catholic now, Father?"

I said yes. He sighed a long, windy sigh and then he relaxed. He was completely at ease. I went back to the rectory saddened over his imminent death and happy to have saved a soul at the very last moment. He died that night, and three days later, he was buried from a Catholic church on Knox Avenue in Grantwood. He received all the honors of a life-long Catholic, with solemn Requiem Mass and commitment in consecrated ground. His wife and his daughters were overjoyed, even in their grief, and some of his Catholic neighbors were puzzled at all the ceremony because, as they said, "The guy wasn't even Protestant. He had no religion."

Most of the marital disputes which come to the rectory belong there. If ever a priest is at his finest with his parishioners, it is at a moment when domestic blissing has been replaced by domestic hissing. One of the cases I recall had me chuckling for days afterward.

It concerns Jimmy and Elinor Townsend. Both were young, and both were in love with each other, although both permitted an exaggerated pride to cloud their devotion now and then. When they walked into my study, they weren't even talking to each other. Elinor was a pretty girl, with dark hair and eyes the size of ten pounds of onyx. Jimmy was tall and slender, and his hair fell over his forehead like Jimmy Stewart's. Before they arrived, I had understood that they were coming to me prior to a final split-up. Both had made up their minds that a separation was inevitable, and each had loudly proclaimed to neighbors that the only way that sanity could be maintained was to get rid of the other party.

They sat on opposite sides of my desk, and I looked to the lady first and asked what the trouble was.

"Father," she said, "it's very simple. I'm a slave. He never takes me out."

"She's a liar," Jimmy said quietly.

"Never," Elinor said. "Never, never, never."

"You keep quiet," I said to Jimmy. "I'll hear you later." I looked at the girl. "Go on."

"It doesn't sound like much, Father, when I say that I'm sick and tired of looking at the four walls. But it's the meanness in him that almost drives me crazy. He works steady. He makes pretty good money. But when I ask him to take me out to a night club now and then, he flies off the handle and curses and he calls me names and—I just can't stand it any more."

I looked at Jimmy for rebuttal, but he just nodded. In sum, what Elinor said was the truth.

"When was the last time he took you out," I said.

Elinor thought a minute, looking at the ceiling.

"Three months ago," she said.

I turned to Jimmy sternly. Before I could say a word, he said, "That's right, Father. And I have no intention of taking her out."

Matters became a bit thick at this point. Elinor was screaming at her husband, and Jimmy was roaring at her. I felt like a spectator at a tennis match, my head swinging to listen to her, then turning to listen to him, then back to Elinor again.

20

I held up both hands for silence. After each one, in turn, tried to get in the final word, they subsided.

Then I asked Jimmy what he had to say. His temper was under such bare restraint that his nostrils flared when he breathed.

"For two years, Father, she's been crying for a Buick. A Buick Roadmaster, nothing less. I make sixty-five a week. That's a Plymouth salary, Father. Not a Buick salary and certainly not a Buick Roadmaster salary. I tried to talk her into a cheaper car; I told her that any car will get her to where she wants to go, but she had her mind made up. Roadmaster or nothing. You know how a woman can nag, Father?" He studied me for a moment. "No, I guess you don't. Well, I got it at breakfast and I got it at supper, and she'd sit at the window and tell me who was passing by in a Roadmaster, and she just never stopped. That's for two years. So you know what I did, Father? I went without lunches and saved money. Lots of times, I walked home from work. I saved here and I saved there. On Saturdays I even did a little extra work to make a few bucks. When I had the down payment on the Buick—excuse me," he said sarcastically, "Roadmaster —I put it down and drove it up in front of our flat and brought her down to see it. We had no right having it, but she wanted it, and I got it. I was in hock up to my eyebrows, but my wife was happy.

"Was she? The hell she was—excuse me, Father—the heck she was. Now she wanted to go night clubbing. I told her she didn't have a Chinaman's chance. All of our money had gone into the Roadmaster, and from now on, when we could afford gasoline, we'd take a little ride, but that's all. When she heard that, she said I could keep my old car, that she didn't want to ride in it. What good was it, she said, if it was only going to sit at the curb? I told her she should have

21

thought of that before she began to whine about a Road-master."

I looked at Elinor. She had started to cry. Her head was down near her lap, and silent sobs shook her shoulders. Jimmy saw it, too. He stopped talking. He looked at her, and then he looked at the study rug and began to press the balls of his thumbs together. Elinor's sobbing was no longer silent. Jimmy made a grimace. An altar boy knocked on the door and said that evening devotions were over and that one of my curates wanted to see me. I told him "in a minute." Elinor was wailing now, but I made no move from my swivel chair. It was not my place to comfort her, and besides, if Jimmy did it, they wouldn't need my help. I know a thing or two about making up. So I waited.

Sure enough, Jimmy took it as long as he could, and then he stood slowly and walked over to Elinor and tentatively patted her shoulder. She cried louder. Then he put his arm around her, obviously embarrassed at my presence. Elinor turned to Jimmy, her eyes ruddy and her make-up ruined, and flung her arms around her husband and kissed him wildly. At this point, I was about as necessary to their existence as one more Buick. Jimmy amazed me, because he started to cry too.

I waited for the tears to stop, and then I looked at both of them sternly. Jimmy moved his chair close to Elinor's, so that he could hold her hand beneath the level of the desk, where I couldn't see. I asked them when they had last been to Mass and the sacraments. It turned out to have been a long time ago. I told them that, if they made their peace with God first, they'd find more peace in the home.

They took the advice. Today, the Buick still stands at the curb, a little old, a little beaten. But not Elinor and Jimmy. They're young and radiant.

You can see, from all this, there have been tragic moments and amusing moments and frightening moments but never dull moments. Still, if you were to ask me, quickly, where my greatest pride lies, I'd have to say in my altar boys. We've had hundreds and hundreds of them, big ones, little ones, fat ones, thin ones, freckled ones, fresh ones, quiet ones, fighting ones—oh, all kinds. My pride is in the fact that over twenty of our boys, in my time at St. Michael's, have become priests.

And sometimes they were the most unlikely kids you ever saw. The very boys I was certain would never never have the call to the priesthood were often the young men who made the finest priests. I don't know why this should be, but it is. It isn't always like this, but I've seen it happen so often that I'm no longer surprised to learn that the dirty-faced kid of yesterday, the villain who poured sneezing powder in the holy-water font, is the hard-working, hard-driving, serious priest of today. Any priest will tell you that it is almost impossible to pick out, from the ranks of the boys, which ones will get the call. Almost all the boys, when they're young, think they want to become priests later in life. That's part of the early piety on the altar. But, later on, they become acquainted with the material things of life, and the Church no longer looks as attractive as it once did. That's natural. Some must save souls, and some must be the souls to be saved.

Of all the boys who became priests in St. Michael's, the one I dwell on most frequently is Ogden Dates. Ogden didn't stand a chance of attaining holy orders. His father, John Dates, boasted to the world that he would never remove his hat in the presence of any priest. And when you get that kind of propaganda at the supper table, the son, who is imitative of the father, cannot be disposed kindly toward the Church.

Ogden's closest friend was Frank Sheridan. They were as

close as Mike and Ike or the Katzenjammer Kids. So, when Frank decided to become an altar boy, Ogden was most unhappy. He wanted to be with his pal in all things, but serving on the altar, with the knowledge of his father, was impossible.

Still, little Ogden brought the matter up at the supper table and waited for the explosion. It never came. His father just looked at him as though this particular child was some strange species which he didn't understand. Ogden's mother, who was Catholic, beamed at her son.

So Ogden studied to serve on the altar, and he and Frank Sheridan drew the eleven-o'clock Mass on Sundays. The boys weren't serving more than two Sundays when I was surprised to see that rousing anti-Catholic, John Dates, at Mass. Lest anyone get the wrong impression, he made it known to everybody that the only reason he was there was not to attend Mass, but to watch his son on the altar. He still had a spitting contempt for the Church, but it swelled the old man's heart to see his son on that altar. John Dates never missed a Sunday eleven-o'clock Mass after that. The more he attended, the prouder he felt. It got so that he knew every move made on the altar, and its symbolism.

One evening the rectory bell rang, and the housekeeper said that there was someone to see me. I walked downstairs, into the study, and there stood John Dates. I smiled. I didn't know what else to do. I looked at his head quickly. It was bare. His hat was in his hand. Gruffly, he asked me if he could receive instructions to become a Catholic. Twice as gruffly, I said sure. In time, John and I became the best of friends. Under the rocks of his personality, he was all shiny gold.

Years later, his son Ogden, and Frank Sheridan, became priests. Don't let them tell you that fathers never weep.

2

B UT BEFORE I tell you more of my recollections about my church, it would be wise, I guess, to tell you something of myself—who I am, what I am, and, most important of all, why I am.

There is a place in Paterson, New Jersey, called Pearl Street. There is nothing to distinguish it from the millions of other small-town streets throughout the United States of America. One of its most undistinguished features is that I was born on Pearl Street on March 12, 1894, in a two-family house. I was the second son of James McWilliams and Henrietta Hall McWilliams. At the time, my brother Raymond was fourteen months old. James would follow me in four years.

At baptism I was christened LeRoy Edward, undoubtedly because my mother, a darling little woman, liked the name and that settled that. My father was the head of the family, just as my mother was its heart. And, because all of us are more creatures of emotion than of reason, the heart was more persuasive than the head. So it was LeRoy. Names aren't too important anyway. It's what you do with the name you have that really matters, and it makes you what you are in the sight of God.

My father was an Irish Catholic, a great man even in retrospect. My mother was an Episcopalian of English extraction. After old Dean McNulty of St. John's had married them, Jim McWilliams found himself with not only a God-fearing and lovely wife, but a most competent housekeeper as well.

It is difficult for me to transmit, in words, what a fine mother she really was. I can say "fine" or "great," but that will not tell you. The promise she made, at her marriage to Jim, to bring up all her children as Catholics was scrupulously kept. So scrupulously, in fact, that two of her three sons were ordained as priests. It was the influence of our mother—an Episcopalian—that made us priests.

Her nickname was "Fairy," because she was so tiny and light that she gave friends the impression of one who has come from an elfin kingdom. The nickname lasted all her life. My father looked like a giant standing beside her. He wasn't really. He was a half-inch short of six feet, a big Irishman with a kindly face and a trusting soul. Jim believed in everybody, and I like to think that everybody believed in Jim.

My reporter friends tell me that nothing is deader than yesterday's news. Maybe so. Maybe not. At the moment, I have before me an editorial published in the Paterson *Evening News* in July of 1932—a long while ago. To me it is still alive, still worth reading.

"When death this morning sealed in eternal sleep the eyes of James McWilliams [it reads in part] there went to a place

26

of glory on high the soul of as fine a man as ever lived in this community.

"Jim McWilliams was the soul of honor, a patient, unselfish religious man who recognized his obligations to God and to man, and who met and performed them in a manner that made him an outstanding example of what a truly fine gentleman and citizen should really be."

I'm glad that I didn't write those words. It sounds so much more authentic coming from someone else.

When I was four, we moved to a new house my father had built on the east side of Paterson—an undeveloped but rapidly growing section. His salary when he married was eighteen dollars a week, and it couldn't have been much greater when we moved. Still, he built the house and got a mortgage on it for less than five thousand dollars. This dwelling still stands on East 25th Street between Broadway and Fourteenth Avenue, and my younger brother James still lives in it.

The parish we lived in was St. Joseph's. It was about a mile from the house, and the pastor, in those days, was Father Charles Gillen, a saintly man with a snowy beard. He was forever appealing for money, and he had good reason for it because his church was destroyed in a great fire in 1902. The church was in ruins, and Father Gillen somehow managed to build a finer church on the ashes. Still, the parishioners told stories about his appeals for money, and one I especially remember concerns a little boy who was crying on Market Street. A passer-by asked what the trouble was.

"He swallowed a nickel," someone said.

The passer-by smiled. "That's no problem," he said. "Just take him to Father Gillen, and he'll get it out of him."

As a boy, I went to Public School 13. The Catholic school was a mile away, and P.S. 13 was only two blocks away.

27

There I was taught by Miss Kelly, a motherly person whom all the students loved. At her marriage six years later, I was asked to be the white-ribbon boy, and I felt honored. My job was to remove the white ribbon on special pews to admit special guests, and then to put it back in place. Everything went smoothly until I became tangled in the white ribbon, and the harder I tried to straighten it out, the more enmeshed I became, until I fell down. The ushers had to get me out of that mess.

My biggest interest those days was sports. Across the street from our house was a lot a city block long. It was there that I learned the fundamentals of baseball, football, soccer, and a game called "kick-the-stick." The stick was a short piece of rubber hose which was placed on the lip of the curb. Many a night, from after supper until dark, we played it. The batter would "kick the stick" and run from home to first base to second base and back home again. If you knew how to kick that "stick" you could send it flying for yards.

I was almost always the smallest youngster in class, and today I do not quite reach five and a half feet; so, to impress the bigger kids, I had to learn faster and play harder. Many a time, in football, the quarterback would say, "On the next play, give the ball to McWilliams, pull his helmet down over his eyes, aim him, and let him go."

If there is any vanity left in me, it's about sports. My great pride was that I seldom failed to make a team I wanted to play for, and most of the other, bigger boys, looked "up" to me. I never tolerated cursing in my presence, but I'm sorry to relate that I did tolerate a bit of stealing. In fact, I participated in it. At Halloween each year, we stole barrels for a big bonfire. End on end we piled the barrels until we had a huge pyramid. Many of the adult neighbors came out to

28

see the blaze, except, of course, those whose barrels were missing.

It sounds funny now, but in those days it was the fashion to wonder, at the age of twelve or thereabouts, what you were going to be when you grew up. The parents wondered too. And, at that time, phrenology was classed as a science. So Raymond and I were taken to Fowler and Wells on East 22d Street in New York. These men had the power to feel a skull and tell what was going on inside. Whether the "science" is real or spurious, I do not know to this day, but I do know that they managed to hit enough truths about a youngster to make the whole business credible to the parents.

I was so deeply impressed with this performance that now, almost a half-century later, I can hear the man talk as his fingers probed my head.

"This lad has been endowed by nature with a good constitution and will therefore be able to generate life in whatever he does. He will throw a healthy influence around him, and were he to become a physician he would have more practice than he knows how to handle. He will not have many patients die on his hands, for he possesses magnetism and is able to inspire the confidence of others. . . .

"His mind is a vigorous one. In fact, he is quick to see the profit and loss of things" (an item which should be of interest to some of my old-time parishioners).

"He would make a very good promoter and an excellent politician of the conscientious type." (Can it be that I'm telling too much, too freely?)

The priesthood, or the ministry, were not referred to, for what the Holy Ghost would do some years later was far beyond the scope of the phrenologist at the moment. There was, within me, a mystery which no one saw at the time.

For me, the first truly religious moment occurred when I was preparing for my First Holy Communion. One day I was trying to memorize the answers to the catechetical questions, and on the next I felt that a great tapestry had been pulled aside so that I could look "inside." The eternal truths attracted me as nothing else had. Suddenly, salvation became the touchstone. Nothing else was of great importance.

First Communion was transmuted overnight into a world-shaking event. I seemed suddenly to know that this thing was all-important—it was the answer to everything and anything; the mere understanding of it could constrict my throat until I felt like weeping, for joy. Nothing, before or since, has had that terrific impact on my life. I felt, somehow, that no one else who was taking instruction with me at that time felt the same deep shaking, down inside, nor did they feel the awful humility which seemed to possess me and own me. I remember reading once that Napoleon said, in his declining years, that the day of his First Holy Communion was the greatest of his life. I understood.

Overnight, I became a revolutionary for Christ, a spiritual rebel for the soul. Father Henry Coyne, then a curate at St. Joseph's, was in charge of instructing the boys. He fired our imaginations, exalted us. He lighted the dimness of heaven and hell, purgatory and the Last Judgment, so that faith became a live thing to be looked at and studied. He made us understand, so clearly and superbly, that when Christ murmured, "What doth it profit a man if he gains the whole world and suffers the loss of his soul?" that there was nothing left of value in the world except faith. The effect of this on a pliable young soul is nothing short of terrific.

Blue suits, white ties, starched collars, white arm bands, and shiny black shoes were the outward trappings of the human boy who was to meet the Divine. We looked good.

Making our first confession the day before was an ordeal. We studied each of the Commandments over and over and over again, trying to understand the full ramifications of each one, but what we really understood was that the greatest evil in the whole world was mortal sin and a tragic end awaited anyone who died in that state.

That first confession is really something. You pile up all the moral debris that has accumulated since you first knew the difference between right and wrong, and you walk into a screened box and you lay it before your Father in Christ. Every wrong you have ever committed, and the number of times you have committed it, is conscientiously exposed. Your confessor is both judge and jury, but you know that from him always comes mercy and pardon. Behind the raised arm of the priest as he pronounces absolution is the raised arm of Christ, just as the words *"Ego te absolvo"* are uttered in His name by the servant of God who uses the priesthood as the medium for the forgiveness of sin.

To me, the great gift of that time was my mother. She took me over my catechism again and again, making sure that I knew the answers. She also helped me to examine my conscience correctly before making that first confession. Maybe my poor writing has not given you sufficient examples of her greatness, but if you can imagine her, after a hard day's work, sitting in the kitchen across the table from me, asking the endless questions over and over—questions involving a religion in which she did not believe—maybe you will understand my pardonable reverence for her. She did as much for my brothers too.

Confession was established as a washing of the soul two thousand years before anyone heard of psychoanalysis. If you have ever made a good confession, you know the peace and serenity it brings. It is the psychiatry of God. It is also a formula for peace that never has been and never can be equaled. God, Who made man, knows what's in him and knows how to prescribe properly for him. Confession strengthens the weak and rehabilitates the wrongdoer.

There's turmoil in the world today because God's plan for man's life has not been accepted. We should take what God gives us, because we belong entirely to Him. Nations fail because they build without God. Only in the Divine remedies will be found peace of mind and soul.

The key to the puzzle is just that simple. It is so obvious it eludes us.

Of course I did not understand these things at the time of my First Communion. Oh, no. The great simple truths take time to comprehend. My greatest concern, at that time, was to be sure that I had prepared a proper sanctuary in my heart to receive our Divine Lord. I had made an honest and sincere and humble confession, and after supper that night, my one thought was not to forget to abstain from all food and drink from midnight until after Communion. Also, I must remember to swallow the Host immediately.

The great day dawned, and with the other youngsters I heard Mass and, at the proper time, stepped slowly up to the altar and received from the consecrated hands of the priest the body and blood, soul and divinity of my Lord and my God. Then I returned to the pew to give thanks as best I could for the great work He had wrought in me.

I felt awfully near to God. Outside the day of my ordination, I can recall no moment that gave me a more heavenly lift. Just as when the Lord took Peter and John to the top of a high mountain and allowed them to glimpse something of His Divinity and caused them to exclaim, "O Lord, it is good for us to be here"—so on the top of my little mountain at

First Communion I experienced an exaltation of spirit very difficult to describe.

Shortly afterward, I became an altar boy. I recognized it as a great privilege to be permitted to serve close to Him. You began as an apprentice, and as you advanced in age and merit, you were given more important duties and functions in the sanctuary and around the altar. The induction ceremonies were impressive. As we were invested in the cassock, the priest said, "Receive this cassock with respect, for it is part of the livery of a soldier in the service of Jesus Christ." And, in bestowing the white surplice, he said, "Receive this surplice, and may its color be a sure sign of the gleaming purity of your soul."

The mechanics were there to produce a model Catholic gentleman, a boy of prayer who was taught to think high, speak high, and walk high, a boy who was enjoined to be kind, respectful, and helpful to all, a boy who must be finer in every way so as to merit the dignity of his work.

It was a question of *"Qui potest capere, capiat"* (let him benefit who could). You had now been exposed to the sunlight of God's favor and grace, and there was no one to blame but yourself if you failed to profit from it.

Strangely, many years later, one of my first assignments as a priest was to be responsible for the altar boys in the Horseshoe section of Jersey City. Imps they were—yes, and we can say it again—they were imps. The boys of Jersey City were tough enough, but they could take lessons in toughness from the "cassocked saints" of Chicago, as we will learn later.

When I graduated from elementary school, I went to Paterson High School. This was a radical change for me, a turning point in my life. Here I was thrown in with young

33

men and women from all parts of the city, of all faiths. I realized the presence of new pressures and influences. I had left a sheltered atmosphere, where I knew everyone, for a world of semiadults, most of whom were strangers. I had been taken from a small pond and dumped into a vast sea.

The best fun of high school, for me, was baseball, swimming, basketball, and football. In football, I was on the Paterson High Seconds, and our toughest opponent was Ridgewood High. They beat us early in the season, 5–0. On Thanksgiving Day, we played a return game at Idlewild Park, just beyond Passaic Falls. Our game was the preliminary one, and in those days all the sporting fraternity of Paterson came out to see the games and celebrate the windup of the season.

Ridgewood scored a touchdown but failed to kick the goal. In some way, they had learned our signals, and they blocked practically every play we started. Then we began to run out of time. There was only five minutes left, and the score was still 5–0 against us. We had the ball on our own twenty, and, at the time, I was quarterback. I called for a play around right end, took the ball from center, and stood still as the whole Ridgewood team swung to our right side. Then I swung to the left and ran the ball—in one of those motion-picture finishes—down the whole field for a touchdown. Taylor, our fullback, kicked the goal and we won 6–5. I felt good about the goal and winning the game, but a little reflection later on proved that I was not too smart. When I first realized that Ridgewood had stolen our signals, I should have known enough at that time to start calling a play, and then to double-cross them by running around the other side.

I realized, at this time, that I was growing up. I felt it, and I knew that I had to begin laying the groundwork for whatever life I was going to lead. I was conscious of new urges unfelt before, and, most important of all, I now understood the reality of sin.

In that high school were young men and women of every race and faith, and many of them, I know now, were God's noblemen. And yet, wrongdoing was rife, and a boy would have to be very stupid not to know it. In fact, after the Ridgewood game, one of the Ridgewood stars invited me to go out with him, and two female friends whom he described as lovely and "accommodating."

This brand of knowledge was shocking to me. I had been brought up in a "hothouse" atmosphere, and now I was being exposed to chillier temperatures. (Maybe that figure of speech is reversible.) In any event, it was difficult for me to reconcile my teachings with what was going on.

And yet, it was out of this clash between idealism and the world of reality that my vocation was born. Because I could not choose both, I had to accept one and renounce the other. I didn't realize it, but this was the first big test of faith. And one morning, before class began, I talked with a kid named Kirwan who sat in front of me. He said that he had just finished a mission in St. Agnes' Church and that one of the missioners had assured him that, if he became a priest, he would be more certain of his eternal salvation than he would as a layman.

Kirwan's little speech coincided with the conviction that had been forming in my own mind. I had already been convinced that the salvation of the soul was everything and that anything else was nothing; so, following that line of reasoning, my place was within the bosom of the Church.

I said nothing to anyone. I was just a worried boy, pondering the eternal mysteries, the mysteries which have engaged the greatest mentalities of all the ages. When I had made up my mind—without prompting or counsel—I next visited

Father Paul Guterl, first assistant at St. Joseph's. Father Guterl was middling in height and had a pleasant face that was somewhat pock-marked. He was of German extraction but looked Italian, and he was easily offended. I told him how I felt. I sat with him, wringing my hands and babbling, trying to justify my decision without knowing whether the Church would want me or not.

When I finished talking, Father was gentle. He asked me a few questions designed, I guess, to test the firmness of the decision. From that moment on, Father Guterl encouraged me and gave generously of his friendship and his counsel. Strangely, others are priests today because of Father Guterl. I don't pretend to know them all, but I can mention as some of his boys Father Joseph McDonald, now paster of St. Charles, in Newark, New Jersey, and Monsignor Carmel Scanlon, pastor of my old parish, St. Joseph's in Paterson, and Father Frank Turner, now pastor of the Church of Saints Cosmos and Damian in the Erie Diocese of Pennsylvania.

The friendship of Father Guterl was of prime importance to me. Just as he never forgot me, I never forgot him. He died a few years ago at St. Paul's, in Clifton, New Jersey, at around seventy. He was an accomplished musician, and he made musical history in Paterson over thirty years ago with his production of many of Victor Herbert's operettas.

While I was talking about Father Guterl, I did not intend to give the impression that I had not confided, promptly and completely, in my mother and my father. I told them of my feelings about life and eternity, and I asked for their approval. It was given at once, unequivocally. And yet I knew that their approval would impose additional hardships on both of them because, a year earlier, my brother Raymond had made the same decision and had dropped his New York job

36

to start his studies at Mt. St. Mary's College in Emmitsburg, Maryland. In later years, I learned from an old friend of my father's that he had to borrow the money to pay my expenses—but I never heard a word of this from my father, so great was his respect for the priesthood and so fearful was he of discouraging me.

3

The remaining steps were difficult. I attended Seton Hall College, beginning in September, 1911. Not all the students were studying for the priesthood. At the start we all took the same courses. Of course you now know my weakness, and it will come as no surprise that I played end and quarterback on the football teams.

I knew that there would be little chance, later on, for me to participate in sports, so I gorged myself, as a stout person might do the night before starting on a diet. I won the fancy-high-diving crown in the Passaic Valley contest, and in my third year at Seton Hall I managed the varsity basketball team. Still, as Catholic boys, we were not always above reproach. I remember arriving in the gymnasium just before a basketball game with New York University, and there stood a great star from St. Benedict's donning one of our uniforms.

As manager, I protested, not only because it was unethical and plain dishonest, but because someone on the opposing team would be sure to recognize him. I was overruled. And someone from NYU did recognize the player, and for years afterward Seton Hall was blackballed by New York University.

In those days, Father J. C. McClary was vice-president of the college and moderator of athletics. Now, even though I was manager of the basketball team, every decision of mine was subject to his approval. Father McClary was always an outstanding priest, but it could not be said that he squandered the college treasury. When I told him that Colgate University would like to play us, he advised me to accept and to guarantee them fifty dollars. They never answered the letter, no doubt because they were stunned by the way we tossed money at them.

Many years later, when Father McClary—then the Right Reverend Monsignor J. Clarence McClary, vicar-general of the Archdiocese of Newark and pastor of the fine parish of St. Aedan's in Jersey City—met me, he would say:

"Roy, do you remember when Colgate . . . ?"

And I would grin and say, "Do I? How could I forget?"

The faculty at Seton Hall was noteworthy, but, as students, we had our fun kidding them one by one. For instance, Father Thomas McLaughlin, a walking encyclopedia and the personification of respect for his superiors, was stout. So we called him "Slitz"—never, of course, to his face. Later, he became the first bishop of Paterson, but his great gift was not teaching. His job was to blue-pencil assignments, and how that pencil whirled! No matter how good the work submitted, Slitz lacerated the sentences until the papers looked like a cross section of the venous system of a frog. One day two of the local wits submitted, as papers, direct quotations from *Ben Hur* and from Cardinal Newman. Sure enough— when they were returned, Slitz had mangled the imperishable

39

prose so badly that only surgery and a plaster cast would fit them together again.

So, we asked ourselves: If Newman and Wallace got the works, what chance did we stand?

Father Dauenhauer taught history and economics. He was kind, genial, a general favorite with all the boys. Yet he was never known to us by any other name than "Dingle." In later years, he became vicar-general of the Paterson Diocese. And Father Frank McCue was called "Balsy" because he wore a wig. Later, he became a monsignor, rector of St. Patrick's Cathedral in Newark. His forte was the ability to simplify a problem. If, when you left his class, you didn't know the answers, it certainly wasn't Balsy's fault. And he kept his simple poise to the end, too. As he lay dying, he summoned his old friend Father Barrett, and named the ministers he wanted at his funeral.

There was Father Cloherty, the best of all the teachers. He had been a Christian Brother, and, rather late in life, he decided to study for the priesthood. If any man could ever say, "Teaching is my business," Father Cloherty was the man. Still, we called him "Pop" all the time, but it was intended as a term of affection. He died before I was ordained, and may God be good to his soul.

There were others, some with nicknames, some without. Father John Duffy, who taught English, was one of the greatest. He knew Genung, the standard guide to rhetoric at that time, from cover to cover, and I believe he could recite the entire work from memory. He was one of the most impressive speakers in the East, and by his silences alone he could compel you to listen.

Like the rest of us, he too had a weakness. It was sensitivity. In his class, anyone who asked a question risked being drawn and quartered because Father Duffy looked upon all such interruptions as a clever plot to trap him. The sarcasm that followed a question would scorch the paint on the classroom walls. In all, though, he was a great ecclesiastic, and the Church rewarded him by making him bishop of Syracuse and of Buffalo.

Another distinguished teacher of my time was the Reverend Mr. Lawlor, who was still a deacon when he took over the freshman-English class. As fine as he was before ordination, he became greater later. He was still a curate when he was appointed superintendent of schools in the Diocese of Newark. The work he did for the children in Catholic schools was so much appreciated that he still holds the same position, even though today the diocese is an archdiocese, and even though he is pastor of St. Mary's Church in Bayonne, New Jersey (a full-time job, I assure you) and even though he is a monsignor and a prothonotary apostolic.

Yes, we had some great teachers. More great ones than not-so-greats. And they turned out good priests. Anyone who attended Seton Hall at that time will tell you that you were turned out as a good priest, or you were turned out.

The men of the faculty were great, and they were tough too. They could not afford to be lenient. Only the brave and the durable and the obedient are worthy of consecration, and at times it seems to a seminarian that the faculty is doing everything in its power to discourage young men who want to be priests. There is a reason for that: the student may have a good mentality and a strong body, but he may have a weak soul. It isn't easy to assess a soul when all that you can see is good test papers, a good physical frame, and a quiet disposition. No church can afford a bad minister. One bad deed on the part of a cleric will get to the ears of many more persons than the pious preachments of a thousand priests. And the one deed will be remembered longer.

Some of the laws imposed upon us as college students were, to my way of thinking, witless. For instance, we had four prefects of discipline—one for each class—and, on our day off, Thursday, the biggest treat we were permitted was to take a long walk with the prefect. It may have been a holdover from ancient seminarian discipline, but I can tell you that it was no fun. Still, when Thursday came, we marched two by two with the prefect up hill and down dale, not knowing whither we were going nor, what is more important, "whyest."

Still, it was not the prefect's fault. He was as much under orders as we, and he was responsible to the president of Seton Hall for everything that happened to us, awake or asleep. In fact, contrary to what you might think, we usually liked the prefect. Genial Jimmy Flanagan, now pastor of St. Thomas Parish in Bloomfield was one of our favorites. If anyone had *excessive* good humor, Jimmy was the man.

But my ideal, the one I wanted most to emulate, was John Clark, the country boy from Hinsdale, Massachusetts. God gave John one of the great gifts, a personality that drew everyone to him. He had tenderness and he had strength, he had humility and holiness, and he had an intellect which stamped him as a born leader of men; the kind of priest all of us aspired to be.

Today, John is Monsignor John Clark, pastor of St. Matthew's Church in Ridgefield, New Jersey, and no one wears the purple with greater dignity. Now, forty years later, he is still my ideal. And I still aspire to be the priest that he is.

The fifty-ninth annual commencement of Seton Hall College was held on Wednesday, June 15, 1915. It was an outdoor commencement. For the first time in my college career, I had attained an honor. I was class valedictorian, and my topic will, I am certain, never become a smash-hit motion picture. It was "The Ethics of the Twentieth Century."

The fervent petitions of the entire class may have been responsible for the rain stopping at 9 A.M. A hot white sun peeped from behind dark clouds, and all the leaves of the trees and the grass glistened. In the wooded area to the west, the first shimmers of heat distorted the landscape. It was going to be a hot day.

Everything went well. Judge Thomas A. Davis of Orange delivered an eloquent address charging all of us to go forward in our vocations, always holding high the ideals of our Alma Mater. There were twenty-three of us that morning, and yet, in those old pre-GI-Bill days, we were the second-largest class to be graduated.

When the ceremonies were over, none of us stood dazedly on the campus, diplomas in hand, wondering, "What next?" We knew. The rector of the seminary had notified us that we were to be accepted. And, in the autumn, all of us would begin immediate, intensive training and study for the greatest of all vocations, the holy priesthood.

The Master had said, *"Duc in Altum"* (launch out into the deep). That's what we were doing. Once we donned the cassock, we had a new life, a life facing the terrifying unknown. Our past lives, our old friends, our family, everyone and everything—all were behind us. We were starting a great new adventure with Christ, and nothing but He mattered any more.

I soon found that being molded into the likeness of Christ is a major operation requiring a lot of self-surgery. I had spirituality, but I also had a lot of self-esteem. And the self-esteem was the first rubbish that had to be tossed out of the attic. My life had to be immersed in His, quickly, completely, permanently. My life, in a sense, had to be lost in order to be found. It wasn't easy.

43

I learned that we cannot seek ourselves and expect to find God. I needed a radical transformation of character, and the only way to attain it was by self-renunciation, by living every moment according to the crucifying standards set forth by Christ in the gospel. There is no other way; there is no compromise; there are no reservations and no short cuts.

That, in sum, was the blueprint of seminary life. Everything else within those walls was subordinate to that. You cannot produce other Christs unless they are prepared to live like Him. Study was only a handmaid to holiness. As Thomas à Kempis said, "I would rather feel compunction than know how to define it." And Domenico Barberi, the Italian Passionist, in England, writing to a superior in Rome in the nineteenth century, said, "Send me over the holy ones rather than the learned ones."

I remember they used to tell a story about two ignorant men walking by Seton Hall. One said to the other, pointing at the buildings, "What's that?" And the other man said, "That's a priest factory."

Crude, but true. Seton Hall was a priest factory. It made and turned out priests. That's where they trained weak and erring men to be God's men. That's where they molded other Christs who would go out into the world to the people to help them in their sorrow, rejoice in their happiness, and above all bring peace and salvation to their souls.

To be accepted for admission to a seminary, as we were, is still not enough to attain priesthood. A careful screening precedes acceptance. And all through the seminary course a minute scrutiny of conduct and attitude is maintained. Just before the conferring of major orders, the banns are announced in the seminarian's home parish to ascertain whether there are any objections from anyone to the ordination. And, again at the actual ordination, the ordaining prelate turns to the congregation and says:

"Should anyone, therefore, have anything against them, let him in God's name, and for God's sake, come forward with confidence and speak. Howbeit, let him be mindful of his own condition."

The physical aspects of the Immaculate Conception Seminary, then located at South Orange, New Jersey, but since removed to Darlington, were far from impressive. It was a three-story brownstone, and in its time it must have been a substantial edifice; but, in mine, I never felt a desire to live there forever.

The refectory was in the basement. The professors had rooms on the second floor and the seminarians on the third. Two students shared each room and shared a gaslight between two desks. The floor was bare. Each student had his own washstand, bowl, and pitcher.

If you roomed in the front of the house, in the winter, you wore a bathrobe as you studied, and it was common to wake up mornings and find ice in the pitcher. There was one room that was colder than all the others. We called it "the freezer." And one sub-zero afternoon, someone hung a red ball outside the door and a sign that said, "Skating here today."

The studies were heavy, harsh, and exacting. And yet, some seminarians, besides their regular work, were asked to do prefect duty in the college, and others were asked to teach classes there in their "free periods." That phrase drew an ironic laugh from many of us, but, for a while, I taught religion and, later on, French. And could you guess where some of my pupils are today? You couldn't. Tom Boland later became Bishop Boland of Paterson and recently, he became archbishop of Newark. Jimmy McNulty is now auxiliary bishop of Newark, and Johnny McNulty, believe it

45

or not, is now Monsignor McNulty, president of Seton Hall University. I hope it is pardonable for me to feel a quiet pride in them—once my boys.

A seminary day is, my friends, a long one. You arise at 5:30, and at 6 you are in chapel for morning prayers and meditation. Your brain is still heavy with sleep, and you are trying to meditate as "Little Napoleon," the rector, walks up and down the dimly lit aisle, and you hope that he will not call upon you to explain the points of the meditation. Your relief is great when he does not call on you, and you know that you are safe for at least one more day.

The rector now goes over the whole meditation, extracting all the spiritual meat from it and making pertinent remarks, or applicable remarks, about current affairs. Mass begins at 6:30. The rector is the celebrant, and everyone receives Communion every morning. Other Masses begin at the side altars. You are careful to make your thanksgiving in the Mass that follows.

At 7:30 you go to breakfast. Afterward you are free until 9 A.M. At that time class begins, and it takes up a large part of the entire day. There are two periods of moral theology and one of dogma. Also, in this day, you study sacred Scripture and ecclesiastical history.

At noon, just before dinner, and in the evening you recite the Angelus. At 3:30 there is a choral recitation of the Rosary, and between 5 P.M. and 6 there is a spiritual reading and a conference by the rector. From 7 P.M. until 9 you study and prepare for the next day. At 9 you go to the chapel for night prayers and meditation.

After that, bed.

I think of this typical day, in its multiple parts, every time I remember a young woman parishioner telling me that she was so nervous that she couldn't sleep "in the afternoon."

46

The one great daring liberty we were permitted was that we could smoke in the recreation room, but we were not permitted to smoke cigarettes. Any seminarian who disobeyed this injunction ran a grave risk. One thing I know: no one ever had to sing a seminarian to sleep.

As you progress in seminary life you are given tonsure and minor orders by the bishop. Tonsure means that bits of hair are clipped from your head, and, at that moment, you are taken from the world and become a member of the clergy. It is called "the making of a cleric," and in the opening prayer the bishop says:

"Dearly beloved brethren, let us beseech our Lord Jesus Christ in behalf of these His servants, who hasten for His love to lay aside the hair of their heads, that He bestow upon them the Holy Ghost, Who shall keep them in the practice of religion forever, and protect their hearts from the stumbling blocks of the world and from worldly desires, so that even as they are changed in outward appearance He may likewise grant them an increase of virtue and opening their eyes deliver them from all spiritual and human blindness and bestow upon them the light of everlasting grace." And then, as he cuts the hair from the head in five different places, each one repeats after him, "The Lord is the portion of my inheritance and my cup; it is Thou that wilt restore my inheritance to me."

The seminarian now bears the likeness of a crown of thorns around his head. He listens to other prayers and invocations by the bishop, who concludes: "Dearly beloved children, you ought to ponder well that you are placed today under the jurisdiction of the Church, and are put in possession of clerical privileges. Take care, therefore, that you do not forfeit these privileges on account of your faults, and strive by a becoming dress, by good conduct, and good deeds, to please

47

God. Which may He Himself grant you by His Holy Spirit, Amen."

The minor orders—porter, reader, exorcist, acolyte—are not a part of the sacrament of holy orders and today are merely a step toward the sacred office of priesthood. These minor orders, in fact, are a carry-over from an ancient ceremony.

During the third year the subdiaconate is conferred, bringing with it the obligation of perpetual chastity. Those of us who belonged to the *profanum vulgus* (hopelessly plebeian) called it the putting on of the tin pants. The daily recitation of the Divine Office from now on also becomes obligatory.

Theologians have disputed whether the subdiaconate is a part of the sacrament of orders. However, the common opinion is that it is not a part of that sacrament. But it is an important step, a most important one. Before conferring it, the bishop admonishes the candidate of its irrevocable nature and charges him to think well, while there is still time to withdraw, on what he is about to do.

In my third year one seminarian withdrew, and it has also happened that a candidate buckled and quit in the sanctuary on the day of the ceremony. In the fourth year the diaconate is conferred, and with it comes greater power in regard to the Blessed Sacrament. With but one more step to go, the ordaining prelate says to the archdeacon, "*Scis illos dignos esse?*" ("Dost thou know them to be worthy?") And the archdeacon answers, "As far as human frailty alloweth me to know, I both know and bear witness that they are worthy of the charge of this office."

And so the ceremony proceeds, solemnly and beautifully, bringing out in detail the nature and powers and obligations of the office. Only the order of priesthood remains before

48

the *sacerdos alter Christus* sets forth to bring Christ wherever he goes.

The kind of priests a seminary turns out reflects, almost mirrorlike, the type of rector who runs the seminary. He is vested with all the authority of the bishop in regard to the seminary, and he literally holds the power of clerical life and death over the seminarians. Under his surveillance you work out your salvation in fear and trembling. The slightest deviation from the rules promulgated by him can, and often does, mean sudden death. He is judge, jury, and supreme court.

Our rector was Monsignor James Mooney. He was short and had large brown eyes and a distant dignity—a dignity that kept you at more than arm's length from him. He was more than a priest; he was a priestly priest. He was never a signpost, pointing the way; instead he walked the way of Christ, and everyone in Immaculate Conception Seminary knew it.

He had a fine intellect, and he was an excellent grammarian. He lived a lonely, isolated life, and he built the walls which kept other people from him. You could respect him. You could feel a reverence for the ascetic life he had chosen. But he never encouraged you to like him. Those who did not like him complained that the Monsignor was on top of Mount Parnassus most of the time. Maybe. If so, he climbed it himself and elected to stay there.

The rector would not fraternize either with the clergy or the laity. When he was with them, he was ill at ease. He had a poor stomach too, and many a night he suffered the pain in silence and read and read and read until the wee hours. Still, the next day, when he chose a walking companion from among the quaking students, the lucky boy almost always heard a wonderful dissertation on a book. Among the walking companions, Bernie Moore was the Monsignor's favorite.

49

Bernie is now the Reverend Bernard Moore, pastor of Sacred Heart Church in Lyndhurst, New Jersey. Bernie had a good sense of humor, good manners, and common sense. It may be that these items were appreciated by the rector.

As he walked, he talked. And as he talked, he coughed. The cough sounded like "pum-pum"; so, as you might guess, he was known to us as "pum-pum Jimmy Mooney." This wasn't intended to be derogatory. Far from it. When he approached, or started a tour of the corridors, he was always kind enough to render the warning "pum-pum," and, if anything was amiss, the boys were now alerted and had a chance to straighten matters out before his arrival.

America was in World War I in 1917, and all laughter left the seminary. We were studying to be priests, to be sure, but we were Americans too, and it was difficult for the boys to read bad news daily and be cooped inside the walls. We wondered and worried every day. To us it seemed as though the world outside were falling apart, just before we were to achieve our greatest joy. Then too, those extra-brilliant seminarians who might have been sent abroad to complete their studies were now kept at home. All foreign publications, such as missals, moral theologies, and breviaries, became exceedingly difficult to buy after April, 1917. When the new Code of Canon Law was promulgated in the following year, only the rector had a copy. So that we could study it, he had to dictate parts of it to us daily.

As students preparing for the ministry, we were exempt from military service, but every day we redoubled our prayers for a cessation of hostilities and for peace throughout the world. Chaplains were being called to service overseas, and the shortage of priests in the Diocese of Newark became so acute that Bishop John J. O'Connor advanced our ordination by six months.

50

After that, matters moved rapidly. We referred to ourselves as "war babies." The Armistice was signed November 11, 1918, and we were doubly thankful that the fire of war had been extinguished before we were ordained. When the news came, everyone was ordered into the chapel, and, under the leadership of the rector, a solemn *Te Deum* was sung.

But that joy was as nothing when, on December 20, 1918, the night before my life's ambition was fulfilled, the rector walked up to me and put his hand on my shoulder. He smiled.

"I have a great gift for you," he said. "Your mother has just been received into the Church."

I couldn't tell you now whether I fell down or wept or just stood there looking stupid. I know that I was numbed. I remember that much. It was all the Christmases rolled into one; all the great joys pyramided into a single event. It was paralyzingly wonderful. Even today I cannot help being overcome in discussing it. To think that He, on the eve of my ordination, would make a gift to *me*, instead of me to Him—well, it was beyond understanding. If she had been there at that moment, I would have hugged her and kissed her, and we'd have danced around the floor—even under the pain of immediate expulsion.

Words are such weak things at times.

That night sleep was difficult. For a time it was impossible. There was so much to think about; so much happiness that I was in delirium. I reflected that, even if I had not become a priest, the education and the training I had received was beyond price. And it was worth all I had gone through to get it. My classmates and I had gone through the fire and had come out purified. The seminary is not for the weak. The conditions under which we studied were more primitive than they are today. I warrant you that no priest-to-be in these days finds himself, in the dead of winter, standing on a chair to keep his feet from freezing.

Now I was about to become a priest. In a few hours, the pink and chartreuse of dawn would be rising in great heavenly suffusion, and then the hour would come. I had achieved a closeness with God that I had never known before. Now I was His man. From this time forward the esteem and applause of men meant nothing. What was important was my growth in sanctifying grace. So far as man was concerned, he would see in me and in my acts the Christus, for now I was to double for Christ. Tremendous powers were about to be entrusted to me, and with them would go very grave responsibilities. I could be great if I put Christ in everything I did, just as I could be a dismal failure if I put myself into everything I did and forgot Him. I fell asleep.

The day came on dragging feet, and the excitement was intense. Deacons were running up and down the corridors, trying to remember the things which must not be forgotten, trying to keep queasy stomachs from bubbling over, trying to feel a tiny bit worthy, but failing, trying to keep the mind from spinning dizzily with excitement. And eventually, after several centuries of time, I found myself in the sanctuary, with the others, standing before Bishop O'Connor.

To appreciate the ceremony of Ordination, one has to witness it. There is a feeling of awe and otherworldness, even among the spectators. The beauty of the prayer of the bishop, as he blesses the hands of the ordinand, is uttered slowly and solemnly:

"Vouchsafe, O Lord, to consecrate and sanctify these hands by this unction and by our blessing. That whatsoever they shall bless may be blessed, and whatsoever they shall consecrate may be consecrated and sanctified; in the name of Our Lord Jesus Christ."

I was privileged, when the ceremony was done, to use those new and holy hands to bless my parents. They had watched everything from the little chapel—Jim and Fairy—and they knelt and bowed their heads in silence for this first blessing. What their thoughts were I shall never know. Pride? Perhaps. Memories? Most probably. Surely they must have thought back to when I was an infant, cradled in Fairy's arms, or to the time when big Jim had to walk the floor with me at night, or maybe to the time, in a carriage in front of the church, when I tossed my bottle out on the sidewalk and the spectators looked at my father as though he were abusing me. Memories, yes. My older brother Raymond was a Jesuit scholastic at the time. My younger brother James was an upperclassman at Annapolis. These thoughts may have run through their minds; thoughts of boys with running noses and holes in their stockings; thoughts of long-ago fevers and little faces hot and dry; thoughts of scrimping and paying bills and doing without; thoughts of their own holy union and their happinesses and what their happinesses had brought forth; thoughts of hardship and laughter and the years which lay ahead, the years, for them, of age and repose.

No one will know what they thought, or even how fast a man and woman can think in the short time it takes for a newly ordained priest to deliver his first blessing. My own heart thumped loudly in my ears; my newly consecrated hands shook; my throat squeezed tight against breathing; I felt completely unworthy to bless Jim and Fairy—my father and mother.

I sang my first Solemn High Mass the next morning at eleven. The weather could hardly have been worse. The cold rain smashed against the big stones of St. Joseph's Church in Paterson, and blackened them. The raindrops walked, in great irregular ranks, down the street. Still the parish, perhaps loyal to its own, turned out in good numbers. Clarence Simoni was an usher. So was Jack Connell, now Dr. John Connell, of Jersey City. My friend, my mentor, my guide, Father Guterl, served as deacon. Another friend, Father Leo Gardner, was subdeacon. My brother Raymond was master of ceremonies. Monsignor Stein, pastor of St. Joseph's, preached a sermon on the priesthood. It was a tender, touching, beautiful thing, and it will live with me forever.

The breakfast was held at the Hamilton Club, and about fifty persons were present, including all the relatives and close friends. Senator Tom McCran, a friend of my father's, was toastmaster. The speeches were few, and there were the usual compliments. But why tell a fellow how great he is when he knows he's a pygmy?

One week later my class reported to Bishop O'Connor to receive our assignments. Ordinarily these assignments are far from permanent. A young priest may serve a year or two, or three or more, in a church, and then find himself transferred to the other end of the diocese. And he may serve in any number of churches before he reaches an age when he is more or less fixed in one parish.

There is another factor. All the new priests know which are the "good" assignments and which are the "bad" ones. The pastor of one church is known to be kindly and easygoing, while another is thought of as a martinet who dismembers young priests before breakfast. The moment I told the rest of the class that I was being sent to St. Michael's Church in Jersey City, they chanted a dour requiem over me in unison.

Did I know Monsignor Sheppard, they asked? I said no. They held their faces in both hands. He was called the "old man," they assured me, and everybody knew that he was the toughest pastor in the diocese. No curate ever lasted at St. Michael's. They went in with head high, and they staggered out in no time to repair their nervous systems in quieter pastures. Sheppard could slay a priest with a glance. A word from him in the pulpit, and the entire city administration trembled. When he scowled, the whole center aisle of the church was emptied out in hurried confusion.

I grinned. If I was about to be butchered, let it be done quickly and mercifully. So I set off for St. Michael's at once. I looked it over from the sidewalk across the street, and I liked what I saw. Moving westward up Ninth Street, I saw a big, old-fashioned convent, four stories high. Next to it was the church, a big, square structure, then about forty years old. Next to that was a new, white-brick rectory, and next to that, the first of many tenements as close together as lips in silence.

4

IF YOU think that I was welcomed by Monsignor Sheppard, you are mistaken. I was greeted by the old housekeeper, who studied me as though she had a suspicion that the Church was becoming lax. She took me up to the second floor, and showed me my suite. It consisted of a study, a bedroom—in the rear, of course—and a bathroom shared with two other curates. The rooms were small, but neat. I hadn't met the Old Man yet, but, no matter what he was like, I was in love with his parish.

The curates' rooms were all on the second floor, in sequence down the hall, so that when the Monsignor came upstairs in the evening, a glance told him whether all his curates were in. He wanted close supervision, and believe me, he got it.

My arrival occurred between Christmas and New Year's Day—the last week of 1918. The following morning I was told that the boss was available and would see me downstairs. He turned out to be big and imposing. He had a leonine head almost completely bald. He sat, in cassock, on his swivel chair, turning gently before his old roll-top desk.

He shook my hand and greeted me cordially. I don't know whether I shook his hand, or just shook. But, whether he was a man-eater or not, I realized I was in the presence of a great churchman, a militant fighter, a personality whose aura filled every crevice in that rectory like incense. He wasn't pastor of St. Michael's. He *was* St. Michael's.

The next thing I learned was that he didn't like to be called Monsignor. Like Francis, Cardinal Spellman, in later years, the Monsignor thought that the highest honor that could be paid him was to be called Father. Another thing I learned in that first meeting was that he had the power to turn the sarcasm on or off at will. When he was contemptuous of someone or something, he could peel the hide off a rhinoceros and dry it, all in one sentence.

When I arrived, he was about seventy and had suffered two cerebral strokes which affected his legs but not his mind or heart. When he walked, he shuffled, and he always said Mass on a side altar. He was "V.G." at the time, which means vicar-general of the diocese, although Father John Ratigan, one of the curates, assured me that it stood for vinegar and gall.

Still, his influence and his power were enormous, inside and outside the Church. He was Bishop O'Connor's strong right arm, and in Jersey City his temporal power was great, too. The strongest politicians came to his door, and waited nervously until the Monsignor was ready to see them. He did not interfere with the day-to-day politics of the town, but woe betide the mayor or the commissioner who was even caught *thinking* of any legislation which might hurt the Church!

I think that secretly he loved a fight, and, when he had

stirred the hurricane, he rode it to victory. Monsignor Sheppard was seventy-five when he sustained his final stroke in Florida, but still he would not lie down and die. He insisted that he be put on a train and shipped to Jersey City at once. Father John Clark, Miss Nellie McCann, and Doctor Ferris hurried down the coast to minister to his needs. He was unconscious on the train, but he seemed to know that he had not yet reached the place where he wanted to make his exit. So he was carried into the rectory on a Sunday at noon, when the rest of us were at dinner. And he stayed alive until three or four the following morning. Then, safely at home, he died. In my estimation, he was the greatest churchman of our diocese. I have not seen his like since, nor do I expect to.

At that first meeting, as he swung gently in his chair, looking me over and looking through me, he said that the forty hours' devotion was going on in the church and that I should go out there and hear confessions.

"Take the confessional on the east side," he said.

No formality. No slow break-in. Just a hello and get to work. I left him and walked through the little corridor which joins church and rectory. The church was big and vaulted, and the edges of the pews were stained light from the thousands of hands which paused there while the worshiper genuflected in slow obeisance to Him Whose home it was. The big pillars of marble looked pale in the feeble light, and the high vaulted ceiling heard the whisper of prayers from far below and echoed them back to the altar.

The forty hours' devotion is a special tribute of homage and adoration, and an efficacious source of blessings for the faithful. It runs through Sunday and Monday and concludes with Solemn Mass and a procession on Tuesday. It is an opportunity for the faithful to draw nearer to God, and confessions are made available to them. As I sat in the confessional box, I knew I was sitting in for Christ and, as my hand was raised in pardon and Absolution, His was raised simultaneously. I had no power, except as He gave it to me. I was His agent, acting for Him and in His name.

I was applying one of the oldest and best remedies for the ills of man. It was a form of psychiatry, but of the Lord's own making, and performed in unbreakable confidence.

When it was over, I remember that the church was cold and it felt good to come to the rectory and get warm. I had received my initiation into parish life, and I hoped that I hadn't done too badly. I was still thinking when the Old Man walked in. He asked me how I made out. I said I hoped all right.

"Good," he said. "Good. Now, there are a few things I have not told you about."

"Yes, Father?"

"A few rules. First of all, I don't want my priests going out on social visits. I don't like it."

"Yes, Father."

"If it is absolutely necessary to pay a social call, I want to know about it. Otherwise, nothing doing. You're here for the welfare of all the people, not just a few. Understand?"

"Yes, Father."

"There will be no going out at night without my permission."

"Yes, Father. How about a sick call?"

"Sick calls are excepted. I will arrange for you to have a day off every week."

"Any particular day, Father?"

"I'll arrange that too. When you take your day off, you check out. When your day off is over, you get in this rectory no later than eleven o'clock. Is that clear?"

"Yes, Father."

"On Sundays I want you to be here at all times, whether there is anything to do in the afternoon or not. You're here at all times on Sunday."

I nodded.

"Now, let me see—oh, yes, marriages. As far as they're concerned, Father Barrett will take care of them and perform them. Of course, if, by chance, he's absent or ill, you may perform them. See me first.

"I don't have to tell you about sick calls and baptisms. You know that they must be entered into the record books the same days as performed."

"Yes, Father."

"That's about all, Father. It takes a day or two to get to know the rules around here."

"I understand."

"Have you seen the hall board?"

"In the outer hall?"

"Come with me, Father." I followed him into the hall. There, on the wall, was a board. Across the top was inscribed: RECTOR—FIRST ASST—SECOND ASST—THIRD ASST. Under each of these was a perpendicular line of holes into which a peg could be placed. Opposite the holes were the words: IN—OUT—CHURCH—SCHOOL.

"This," he said, "is not an ornament. Far from it. I put it here to be used at all times. I want to know, at a glance, where any priest is."

I learned quickly that there were other rules. When a priest left the rectory to go anywhere, he must mark the exact time on the board. When he returned, he must again mark the time. Thus, if I marked "1:06 P.M. sick call" and "2:16 P.M. returned," the Monsignor would wait until the next mealtime and, in the course of supper conversation, ask

60

me what took me so long. The answer had better be highly credible, or else the sarcasm became as warm and dripping as the gravy on the potatoes.

Another rule—all of these can be called ironclad—was that male converts were to receive instruction at the rectory, females at the convent. Also, regarding the convent, none of us were ever allowed to go there to say hello, or to inquire after the health of a sister, or the welfare of a child in school. We went there on official business, or not at all. A telephone which hung on the rectory wall was good only for local calls, and its exposed position was a guarantee of no privacy. The kitchen was called "no man's land," and no priest was allowed in it. The Monsignor was opposed to familiarity, on the part of his priests, with anyone, including the old cook.

Father Robert Marnell, a classmate of mine, once said that what St. Michael's needed most of all were two green lights on stanchions, and then *everybody* would know that it was a police station.

The rules for mealtimes were just as rigid as the others. Breakfast was served at 8:30, dinner at 12 noon, and supper at 6 P.M. The food was plain, but it was also substantial. The breakfast hour had the curates chewing on their own teeth with irritation. The first Mass was at six, the second at seven, and a wait until 8:30 for breakfast was a long time to these men. The boss knew it, but he made the priests wait anyway. He said the 7:30 Mass on the side altar and afterward went for a walk around Hamilton Park in cassock and biretta. When he returned, the bell was rung immediately, and we all sat to breakfast. He always returned from these morning walks with a twinkle in his eye, as though he knew that his young priests had been chafing for breakfast, and knew that their silent exasperation was impotent.

No matter how strongly anger bubbled within us, the

moment the Monsignor sat down to breakfast it dissipated like a morning haze under a strong sun. He was the most engaging host I've ever known, and he could keep conversation stimulated around the table by merely uttering a word or a phrase every now and then. Sometimes he would steer the conversation toward the goodness and piety of the parishioners who attended Mass every morning. At other times, adroitly, he would channel it toward the news of the day. Now and then, he would start a philosophical discussion, and when he had ascertained which side of the question his curates assumed, the Monsignor would take the opposite view. Today, it seems a shame that we did not have tape recorders in those days, because his rich and incisive views are lost for all time.

He would tilt a lance with anyone, at any time, on any subject. Once a few public-spirited citizens wanted to build a golf course on the southern side of the city. No one, except the Monsignor, could find any reason why it should not be built. He found reasons: plenty of them. When he finished reciting his reasons, everybody in town knew that golf was the game of snobs—rich, idle snobs. In the Monsignor's time, no golf course was built in Jersey City.

On another occasion, a county judge moaned that most of the cases of juvenile delinquency that came before him concerned Catholic children. When we curates read that, we let out a whoop. We knew that this would be Monsignor Sheppard's ball to handle. All the other church pastors seemed to know it too, without being told. All of them kept quiet while the boss dissected the judge, limb from sinew, tossed the cadaver on a garbage heap, and then cited chapter and verse about the total number of delinquents of one religion as opposed to others. The attack was so vigorous, the arguments so well founded, that the judge counted himself lucky to live long enough to withdraw his statement. No judge or public administrator was too highly placed for "Old Grizzly" to go after him.

After supper he led us into church and we prayed. Then, if the evening was quiet, we joined him in his large sitting room on the first floor. There the conversation was just as lively, but it was almost always about parish matters. He picked our brains, at this time, about everything that was going on in St. Michael's. No item of observation was too small to be uttered and to receive suitable comment. At these times he was gentle and cordial and helpful, and a young priest would leave the room at bedtime hating himself for ever being exasperated with the pastor.

Still, he could criticize anything and everything without fear or favor. Every evening in the church, there was a recitation of the Rosary and a spiritual reading. He never failed to be in attendance, watching, listening, his eyes darting, his head immobile. When it was over, the priest who conducted the service would hear the comment, "You were too fast," or "You were too slow," or "You were too loud," or "Nobody could hear you." No priest ever got a swelled head in St. Michael's, and none ever felt that he was doing a good job. You may have come into the parish with a small amount of hidden pride, but it was driven out and stamped underfoot by the Monsignor in a week or two.

The curates took turns preaching at the High Mass on Sunday, and every third Sunday it would be my turn. At noontime dinner, you heard the verdict. No matter how eloquent you thought you were, the Monsignor could find flaws in your delivery or your reasoning or your choice of words or your pronunciation. The sad part was that his criticisms were always valid. His criticism of me was contained in seven words: "Let yourself out, McWilliams, let yourself out." He said it many times. I began to think that a compliment would never come my way when, one Sunday at dinner, he said: "You're coming out of your shell fast, McWilliams." That was all, but that was enough. I almost fell off my chair. It held my morale aloft for weeks.

Always, at High Mass, the Monsignor sat in the sanctuary, listening. His reputation as a critic was such that many priests dreaded to be invited to preach at St. Michael's. "Himself" never cared who you were, or what a high reputation you had as a preacher—he listened, and if he didn't like what he heard, he said so and said it loudly.

One year the Holy Name Federation was conducting a triduum for men, and the spiritual directors of the many parishes exchanged pulpits for the moment. We drew Father John Banks, of nearby St. Lucy's. He came over to preach at St. Michael's, and, as he walked into the sanctuary, he spotted the Monsignor. He was so upset, so visibly upset, that he no sooner stepped up into the pulpit than he stepped down and ran.

Afterward the Monsignor frowned and said, "Will you tell me what that man packed his bag for?"

No one told him.

There were other diplomatic incidents: many of them. Years before my time, young Father Michael Mulligan, now a monsignor and pastor of St. Henry's Church in Bayonne, was a curate at St. Michael's, and many a Sunday when Mulligan was preaching, "himself" would get up from his chair in the sanctuary and slam the door leading to the altar loud enough to make thunder echo throughout the church. That was the Monsignor's expression of appreciation. In the last three days of Holy Week, I recall, he watched the ceremonies from inside the sanctuary door, and if he saw you making a mistake, or what he thought was a mistake, he issued an immediate, and loud, correction. Father Jimmy Owens, who is now a monsignor in Nutley, served under Sheppard in the early 1900s, and Father Owens was noted for his placidity. He never got rattled. But, one day, while going through ceremonies as celebrant, he heard a terrific roar come from the "throne." Without pausing in his work, he turned toward the sanctuary and yelled, "Who's doing this? You or me?" The Monsignor subsided with a grunt, and, later, Father Owens took off for greener pastures.

His pet peeve, though, was lights. He was the most efficient light-turner-offer I've ever known, and I've known a lot of them. This is a peeve the Monsignor shared with many other pastors, but I doubt that any of them could match him. The moment a modicum of lights had been turned on for a church ceremony, "himself" would come in and turn them off. This must have confused the parishioners, but it never confused us. The worst I remember was one late afternoon when I was talking to a parishioner in the downstairs sitting room. The man had a problem, and I was listening attentively when I heard the rustle of a cassock and looked up just in time to see the Monsignor walk around the room, without a word, turning each of the lights off.

"Can't see paying all this money to the Public Service Company," he said, and stomped out. After that, I'm sure that the parishioner could see well by the light of my face.

When June was over, all of us knew that we were in for a respite. That was the time when the Monsignor went down to Long Branch, New Jersey, a seaside resort, for the summer. If ever we curates had time for a free breath of air, this was it. Still, after he arrived, his unfailing habit was to phone the rectory every evening. No matter which priest answered, the same two questions floated over the wire.

"Is everybody in?" The answer had better be yes, or else

65

I think he would have flown through the telephone wire. And it was yes, a truthful yes—until after he hung up.

The other question was, "Anything new?"

He loved news. Like the newsreels, he saw all, knew all. He had informants all over the diocese and in different parts of the parish. If we said that there was nothing new, he'd tell us what was new from his summer retreat. We were always in awe that he could learn so much so quickly. The best course to follow was to tell him what was new according to your knowledge, holding back nothing under pain of the coming sarcasm. When he was home, sometimes the Monsignor was not content to wait for the hot telephone to ring with the news, he'd go out and dig it up himself. He would shuffle along the streets in bifocals, leaning on a cane, and he would make regular stops at the Finnertys' on Eighth Street, the Garrys', Currys', and McGoverns' on West Hamilton Place, and so on around the circuit. When he got back to the rectory, he was sagging with sagas. His eyes twinkled with amusement, and sometimes, if he was of a mind, he would spring a little bit of it at supper. Most of it he kept to himself, but the stuff that he felt might be good for our minds, and good for a conversational stimuli, came out at supper.

In the summertime each of the curates got three weeks' vacation. But, before my time, a priest failed to return at the exact moment he was supposed to replace another priest. So what happened? Just what you might expect—from that time forward, for all the years remaining to the Monsignor, each priest still got three weeks' vacation, but he had to return every Saturday and Sunday for confessions and Mass. This can hurt a vacation badly—and it meant that no vacation could be had very far from St. Michael's—but there was nothing we could do about it, and no protest would have been answered with more than a thin smile.

Money is important to the upkeep and the expansion of any church, despite the pious shying away from the subject encountered in many churches. Without it, you haven't got a church. And without a church, you haven't got a parish. So, distasteful or not, the collections had to be counted every Sunday, and the returns had better be bountiful. We used to hope that "himself" would invest in a counting machine so that we wouldn't have to spend hours sorting and stacking the coins. But every time a salesman called to sell one, the Monsignor's old-fashioned stubbornness would assert itself, and he made it adequately plain that he got along for years before there were any counting machines, and he'd still be getting along for years after the machines were gone. The same applied to envelopes for collections. We curates tried to tell him that the envelopes would increase the collections, but he was just as certain that he would not invest money in envelopes.

After the Monsignor died his successor introduced envelopes, and the collections tripled. And today a counting machine reposes in the small office behind mine. I'm sure he would have frowned on the Addressograph machine we have too. If God permitted him to come back for an hour, I know the Monsignor would throw all of them out in the middle of Ninth Street.

He knew how difficult our duties were, but he did nothing to alleviate the situation. Each curate got fifty dollars a month, and that had to cover every contingency. Yet he was not above reminding us of the fifty dollars if we complained. And, on occasion, he could figure a way of making matters worse for us. For instance, the day before Christmas is about as trying a day as you can imagine. As a priest, you hear confessions all afternoon, sometimes from 2:30 until 6 P.M., cooped up in a little screened box. At St. Michael's, usually the three curates heard the confessions of perhaps 800 children. Still, the Monsignor was not above inviting the first assistant out for a drive on an afternoon like that, so that, instead of three priests hearing confessions, we had two. On Christmas Day each of us said three Masses, and, when we weren't saying Mass, we had to assist in taking up the collections. Any priest who had an idea that he might be able to have Christmas dinner with his parents had better have a mental examination. On Christmas afternoon we sat in the record room and counted the collection—*all* afternoon. The Monsignor had gone out riding, visiting the graves of loved ones, and when he returned at about six, we were sore-eyed and weary.

"Well," he would say nonchalantly, "how was the collection?"

In the matter of baptisms, these were supposed to take place at four o'clock on Sunday. But "himself" never permitted us to announce the time. Thus, after dinner on Sunday, the first infant would be carried into the baptistery, and, after the baptism, the priest hardly returned to his quarters before the next one came in. This often went on all afternoon. When we told the boss that it would be simpler to say "four o'clock" and do all the baptizing at once, he waved us away and said nothing doing; we were soldiers of Christ and were supposed to be kept busy at all times.

That will give you an idea of my "boot training" as a priest. When Monsignor Sheppard got through with me, I was as tough as nails and ready for any emergency. I remembered, in seminary, that we were taught, "Egoism must die.

68

It must die daily"; and I now thought ruefully that if I had any left, the Monsignor had certainly shot it out from under me. My ears had been pinned back as close to the skull as possible. My first six years in the priesthood, under the Monsignor, were a matter of training which made seminary life look like a May walk. There wasn't any flabbiness left in my character when God beckoned to the Monsignor to come and give an account of himself. And into the account book, on the credit side, I think he could have said, with justification, "I made McWilliams a better priest than he might have been."

Before he passed on, the Monsignor must have seen in me the love of a good fight, because I found him standing behind me and egging me on when anyone attacked the Church. In those early days, the most zealous anti-Catholic was Dr. James Parker, pastor of the Second United Presbyterian Church. He wasn't content to husband his own flock; he wanted to scatter ours. So, on one occasion, he invited an "ex-priest" to take the pulpit in his church and give his lip-smacking congregation the low-down on priests and nuns. This "ex-priest" advertised himself as the Reverend Patrick Morgan, a onetime Capuchin monk.

When I read about it in the local newspapers, I seethed. The Monsignor saw the fire in me, and he fanned the flames. He waited until I was fairly foaming at the mouth, then he unsnapped the leash and, in effect, said, "Now . . . go get 'em!" I investigated the Reverend Mr. Morgan, and, when my research was done, I attacked him in the press. And I knew that, if I wasn't certain of my facts, I'd be sued, and sued for plenty.

I denounced the good father as a phony. I said that even his first name was cockeyed; it wasn't Patrick, it was Harold.

He never was a Catholic priest and never received any orders leading toward the priesthood, and his vicious fictions about priests and nuns had been disproved again and again.

"As a well-known Canadian journal says," I wrote, "this Hal Morgan (there is nothing Irish about him, thanks be to God!) was expelled from a Franciscan monastery and told that he had no vocation for the Catholic priesthood. He had been a sort of convert to Catholicity for a year or two and was living on the bounty of a good old Irish priest. This can all be proved by documentary evidence any time that someone has the interest to inquire for it.

"Now let me say to you, Mr. Parker, that you are doing neither yourself nor your church any good by having recourse to men and methods of such a kind. To abet and to further bigotry is un-American and unpatriotic, lacking in the first elements of common decency and true citizenship."

After that blast, the Reverend Patrick Morgan invited me to a public debate. I countered with another shot at Parker—who was the real target—and challenged him to answer five pointed questions. I concluded by referring to his protégé as "just one of the weeds flung over the wall from the Pope's garden." After that nothing was heard from either of them.

Another argument which bedeviled the city in the early 1920s was a definition of what constituted the true observance of Sunday. The Lord's Day Alliance stood firm for a puritanical Sabbath and banned all, or almost all, types of public recreation and amusement. They found that the statute books still held blue laws regarding Sunday, even though these laws had not been observed by the people. And the moment that these old laws were discovered, the Lord's Day Alliance insisted that they be observed. As a result, all motion-picture houses were closed on Sunday.

The fight shaped up as anti-Catholic versus Catholic. The

attitude of the Catholic Church has always been that the Sabbath was made for man, not man for the Sabbath. The Church demanded that man worship God by attendance at Mass on Sunday and also suggested other spiritual works, such as attendance at benediction and spiritual reading. In the mind of the Church, however, it did not seem to be sensible to put man in a spiritual strait jacket on his day of rest from his labors. The Lord's day was intended to be a day for man to rebuild himself spiritually and physically. In sum, we saw no harm in wholesome recreation.

The battle was on. The Lord's Day Alliance had one weapon which guaranteed that they would win the fight. The theaters had closed down on Sunday—all of them—and none would dare to open. The only possible way that we could crack the solid front was to try to open one theater. If we could open just one, we knew that the rest would follow. It wasn't going to be easy.

The biggest theater in Jersey City, in those days, was the State, at Journal Square. I decided, with the connivance of the old fox himself, to have the Dramatic Society of St. Michael's Church stage a Sunday performance of *The White Sister* at this theater. The manager, Mr. Bernstein, seemed more than eager to let us have his theater on Sunday afternoon and evening, February 10, 1924. He would not commit himself on the law, but he realized that, if the Lord's Day Alliance couldn't cause us to be arrested, all the theaters would soon open on Sundays.

The two performances were jammed. The eyes of the whole city were upon us, and we played the situation to the hilt. The newspapers gave the story a lot of space, and no one tried to arrest us. At each performance, we gave out circulars which bore the following inscription: "All equal before the law. No discrimination. Rev. LeRoy McWilliams, who stands for True Observance of Sunday as propounded by a member of the Supreme Court of New Jersey Friday Feb. 8, 1924 in his indisputable charge to the grand jury, Hon. James F. Minturn."

The judge, only two days before, in a matter of blue laws and Sunday laws in general, seemed to favor our side in his charge. The Lord's Day Alliance, which was a small, volatile group, quit the fight. The theaters, one by one, reopened. I cannot see how the cause of the Lord can be hurt by permitting people to attend a movie on Sunday. Once their spiritual obligations are behind them, any wholesome fun is good for the whole family.

5

I DOUBT very much that there is any city in this great Union where politics is more important than in Jersey City. It almost seems that every one of the 300,000 persons who dwell here, including the children, is a politician. Politics is to Jersey City what baseball is to Brooklyn. Any man, lounging in a corner tavern, can give you all the answers to the political maneuvering of the hour. And if he isn't on the public payroll, known locally as the "pad," he has a cousin or an uncle or a brother who is. Merely by studying the list of pallbearers at the funeral of a politician, he can tell you who is in favor, and who is out. Every pronouncement from City Hall is studied, and studied again, for the hidden implications. A man in the sanctity of his own home would hardly dare admit to his wife that the Republicans might poll a few votes in the next election, for, if it ever leaked out, it could mean disaster for him.

As a curate in the Horseshoe, I watched the political parade go by. I had a ringside seat, too, because Frank Hague lived in St. Michael's Parish. So did his nephew, Frank Eggers, who succeeded him as mayor. And John V. Kenny, who fought them both and beat them. And John Malone, the man with the shape like a soft-boiled egg, who was Hague's deputy mayor. They were all in St. Michael's, and all I can say in the parlance of the times is—Ohhhh, brothhhh-er!

In a way, Monsignor Sheppard is responsible for Frank Hague. When the tall, skinny redhead first ran for public office, the boss published a few favorable words about him in the parish bulletin. Now Jersey City was, and is, a predominantly Catholic city, and apparently the O.K. of a priest carries more political weight than it should. The Davis machine, then in control of City Hall, assumed that Hague had the blessing of the Church, so it backed him and he won. That started his climb to power: the greatest power a mayor has ever had.

I doubt that the Monsignor, for all his foxiness, could have foreseen that this gangling youngster, whom he had publicly patted on the back, would develop into a genius among politicians and would someday hold the state of New Jersey in the palm of his hand. In fact, years later, when a tearful mother and father came to him in City Hall to ask for help for their son, who was to be executed in the electric chair, they sobbed that the governor would not see them.

"Now, now," Hague said soothingly, "you couldn't be closer to the governor than you are right now."

And he was right. He made and broke governors, senators, commissioners, judges, at his pleasure. Johnny Malone was his deputy, and the two turned out to be one of the greatest political batteries ever known. Hague made the decisions; Malone carried them out, with infinite pains, whether he subscribed to them or not. Working under them, they had twelve ward leaders who learned, to their horror, that it was not enough to turn in as big a Democratic majority as last year's. It had to be bigger. I remember a situation in which the leader of a heavily Democratic ward apologized publicly to Hague because, in one of his districts, two Republican votes were counted. He promised that it wouldn't happen again.

Once Hague started in public life, he realized the value of the friendship and the backing of the Monsignor. And he determined that he would never lack that support, no matter what happened. Hague was shrewd; but the old fox was shrewder. Hague needed Sheppard; Sheppard didn't need Hague. But "himself" played the game with the politician because he had an ax to grind. He noted that there was scarcely a Catholic in any worth-while public job. No Catholics held any of the major judgeships. The Monsignor wanted that situation changed. He didn't want more Catholics in top political jobs than the ratio of population warranted; but he wanted his due. He was working for the Church, first, last, and all the time, and if he could jimmy his way into a position where Catholicity would benefit, the Monsignor would do it.

The Sisters of Charity of St. Vincent de Paul, at Convent Station, owned an old orphan asylum at the corner of Pavonia Avenue and Erie Street. It occupied a whole block and was valued highly as a piece of property. Still, the sisters abandoned the building and moved away. When World War I came along, the building was used, temporarily, as a barracks. After the war, the place became an eyesore.

It was in a situation of this kind that the Monsignor blended politics with good common sense. He suggested to Hague that the spot would be ideal for a public school. He showed Hague, on a map, that the city would have to build a school in the area. The result? One of the finest public schools in

75

the city, P.S. 37, stands today where the old orphanage once rotted, and the mother-general of the Sisters of Charity at Convent Station received a check for $162,500 for their property.

Hague and Sheppard were close, yes. But the Monsignor never permitted the mayor to regard him as anything but a churchman. The Monsignor's clerical dignity was always intact, and when Hague stopped on the street to chat with him, the mayor removed his hat. In the Monsignor's fiftieth year as a priest, and the last one of his life, Mayor Hague started to take up a purse for him. It was a fine gesture, and I am sure that it would have been an enormous purse. But the moment "himself" heard about it, he had it stopped at once. His priesthood was not for sale. Years after the old fox was gone, Hague had a small playground, behind the church, named Monsignor Sheppard Park. It's still there.

When I first went to St. Michael's, the priestly line-up was like this: Monsignor Sheppard, pastor; Father Edward Barrett, first curate; Father John Ratigan, second curate; Father LeRoy McWilliams, third curate. As first assistant, Father Barrett had a great deal of power and authority. You will recall that the Monsignor was also vicar-general of the diocese, and his duties, therefore, took him outside the parish on many occasions. Thus the run-of-the-mine daily decisions were often in Father Barrett's hands, and, in a way, he was our daily boss.

Father Barrett was an unusual person. He had a tremendous physique and a sharp mentality. One side of his character would remind you of violets; the other side, of violence. He could be cordial, and he could be caustic. He seemed to be one of the few persons in the world who were unafraid of the boss, and when he disagreed, Father Barrett would argue with the Monsignor all day long, following him from room to room. Once, the Monsignor turned to him and said, "It seems that I am nursing a viper in my breast." But that didn't bother Barrett, and he was not to be deterred by flattery. He kept arguing the main point of the dispute, and, after supper, the two always became friends again.

Those of us who were inside the rectory, and saw all this, had a suspicion that the old Monsignor relished having a fighter around because, if he didn't, he could have arranged for Father Barrett to be transferred. And you can add to the evidence the fact that the Monsignor reposed deeper and deeper confidence in Ed Barrett, no matter how scathing the daily disagreements.

The second assistant, Father John Ratigan, was as unlike the rest of us as it's possible to be. He was a humorist. He could tell jokes without pause by the hour, until his audience was rolling on the floor. He had a brilliant memory, and after reading something once or twice he could recite it verbatim. He had audacity supreme, and I am sure that if it suited his purpose, he would walk in on a secret session of the college of cardinals. The Monsignor always said, with some acidity, that Father Ratigan's "detectors" were good, but his "reflectors" were bad.

By all counts I was the baby. I was at least ten years younger than anyone in the family. The rest of them gave me no illusions about my humble status, and I was given the least desirable days off too. For example, although theoretically I was supposed to administer to the entire parish, in practice I was permitted to make sick calls only in that part of the parish where I took the annual census. I was made to understand that I belonged to the great unwashed, and that it would be a mark of virtue on my part if I constantly remembered my place.

As assignments, I was given charge of the altar boys, the

Junior Holy Name Society, the Angel and Saint Cecilia Societies, and the Young Ladies' Sodality, commonly known as the Children of Mary. Father Barrett reserved for himself the two major societies: the Holy Name and the Rosary, or married-women's organizations. In those two reposed the heart of the parish. Father Ratigan was moderator of the League of the Sacred Heart.

But these, of course, had nothing to do with the daily duties of a priest. The Monsignor set up a schedule so that a priest was always "on duty" in the rectory. This job, which was the toughest of them all, fell to Father Ratigan and me. As senior curate, Father Barrett was exempt. While on duty I said the six-o'clock Mass every morning, with the exception of the day following my day off, when I said the seven-o'clock Mass. Father Ratigan alternated with me, a week on duty, a week off.

In the outer vestibule of the rectory was a panel of buttons, which, when pushed, rang the bell in one of the priest's rooms. During the day, the bell rang in the kitchen, and the housekeeper would go to the door to see who was there, and then summon a priest if necessary. But at nine in the evening, whichever priest was on duty switched the call button so that it would ring in his room. In the morning, the first priest downstairs would switch the call button back to the kitchen.

The orders given to the housekeeper were that the priest on duty was to be summoned, no matter what the hour. Between 1 and 3 P.M. Father Ratigan and I would try to take a quiet siesta, but it seldom worked out quietly. St. Michael's is not a quiet parish. As I told you, it is full of Irish and Poles and Italians—all people of great vibrance—and a priest never knew what awaited him when he answered the call of the bell. Every type of person walked into that rectory; every known type of problem was presented.

78

One day I was called downstairs and found a young lady of about eighteen sitting there. We had a roll-top desk in those days, and I sat in the chair before it and asked her what I could do to help. I had hardly turned toward her when she jumped up from her chair and planted herself on the desk. She could hardly have been closer. For once, I lost my composure.

"Isn't this just a bit too clubby?" I said.

"Is it?" she asked, and jumped back to the chair.

"What is it, miss, that you want to see me about?"

She smiled engagingly. "I've been thinking, Father, about priests in general. Seriously, I mean. And I honestly feel that it is impossible for a priest to keep his vows."

"What vows, for instance?" I was growling now.

"Well, you're supposed to keep away from women, and it seems to me that it's impossible for any man. . . ."

"There's the door," I said.

"But what I was thinking, Father. . . ."

"Get out."

"If you'd only listen a minute. . . ."

"Get out!"

She got. I never saw her again. Another time, I was summoned and a young man sat waiting. He was the epitome of dejection. I asked what the problem was, and he said that he had to get out of town in a hurry. The police were after him. He had been the driver of a car in a holdup. He wanted to get away quickly. He'd never do it again, but if the police ever laid hands on him, he'd be put away for a long time. I felt sorry for him, and I staked him to a small amount. I found out later that there was no such holdup, and the police were not looking for the sad young man. He just wanted a handout, and he came equipped with a good story.

Another time I went downstairs, and a man bounded across

the room and grabbed my hand. He said that a small, select group of names had been selected, and that I was among them. I was to be honored by being privileged to buy a set of books called *Lives and Messages of the Presidents*. He was so convincing that I felt that I was indeed lucky. I made a down payment and agreed to pay the rest in monthly installments. I still have the books, and I don't think I've ever used a set less than that one. I was born to be a "fall guy," but I console myself that most priests are as bad, or almost as bad, as I. They'd buy ice-cream cones in a blizzard.

I never realized that, in St. Michael's Parish, the parishioners are closely related and that, if you step on one toe, you step on countless others. A young married couple called on me one afternoon to register a complaint. They lived on the fourth floor of a flat and, across the dumb-waiter shaft, the lady next door kept taunting them with the accusation that they *had* to get married. They couldn't stand it another moment, they said. It was destroying their peace of mind.

What would you have done? I wasn't sure. The woman they were accusing was a good woman. I knew that. I didn't want an explosion, so I advised them to go home and pay no attention to what she said. It was a nasty complaint, and I wanted no part of it. Within a few days, they were back. The woman was getting worse. All evening long she hollered her accusation across the dumb-waiter shaft, and surely the neighbors on the floors below must have heard. I didn't like it. But I didn't do anything about it. I sent them away with a promise that, if it happened again, to tell me at once. And they did. When they arrived the third time, the young husband was livid with anger, and the bride was in tears.

I went to see the offender in the afternoon. She greeted me cordially and asked me to sit down and have a cup of tea. But when I tried to reach the point of my visit, I knew at once that McWilliams had been caught off base. She exploded like a fifty-cent Roman candle, in all colors and in all directions. She was humiliated, she said, deeply, irrevocably humiliated to think that a priest would have to call upon her, in her own home, to press a complaint. She yelled louder and louder, and you never saw a black cassock back toward a door with the speed that was in me. I flew.

That wasn't bad enough. At seven the same evening, a big, red-faced Irish woman called upon me personally. Her eyes were on fire and, before she said hello, I knew the story. This woman was the mother of the one I had visited. Stupidly, I hadn't connected the two marriage names. I was in for trouble, and there was no way out. This one was one of the pillars of St. Michael's, a fine woman who had done much for the church.

I wish I could repeat what she said to me, but it came so fast, and with such stunning force, that the words tumbled over each other and telescoped, like a long freight train in a wreck. I do remember her shrieking that sure, her daughter was as good as any woman in the parish, and the idea of having a priest call to make a complaint, the very idea of a priest (etc., etc., ad infinitum, ad nauseum, ad . . .).

I sat and took it. I deserved everything she said. I still thought that the original complaint was justified, but if the aggrieved young husband had only spoken a quiet word to the other woman's husband, if only I hadn't been so eager to be a marital umpire . . . oh, well. A young priest has to learn some of the bitter temporal lessons the hard way. I found out later that the woman's whole family was angry at me. And she had aunts and cousins and nieces and nephews all over the parish.

Another type of call we had at the rectory was the administration of the pledge. In those days, we didn't know that alcoholism is a malady, like diabetes or t.b., and all of us thought that with a little will power Johnny would stop drinking. Some had spent their pay, starved their families, beat their wives, or been arrested. Sometimes the judge would grant a suspended sentence to a family man who promised to take the pledge. So, in the rectory office, we administered it right and left.

One thing I can say in favor of the pledge: in borderline cases where the man was not yet a confirmed alcoholic, it jacked him up at the right time and restored him to a tearful and loving wife and children. It worked, and it worked well.

There was one fellow who, periodically, would ring the night bell at one or two in the morning and demand to see "Pastor" McWilliams. When I got a glimpse of him, I realized that he had on a lovely "package." He would stand in the hall, weaving slightly and smiling, and ask me if I would lend him a "buck." I never refused. And you know something funny? He never failed to return the dollar.

Another character showed up on an average of every two weeks. This man always had the same story. He could get a job in West Nothing, New Jersey, if I would give him the carfare to get there. The first two or three times, he got the carfare. He took the money and danced off to the nearest saloon and got loaded to the brows. After that, I refused to give him the money, but he always tried once more. Finally, I asked him point-blank why he didn't let the stuff alone. He was hurt that I would suggest such a thing. I was assured that I had the wrong man, that he never touched the stuff. When I asked him if he went to Mass every Sunday and if he had made his Easter duty, he assured me that he had. He was the very soul of Catholicity. There was no real harm in the man, but he had no spine. Not so long ago, he became ill and died. He had spurned God, but God didn't spurn him. God gave him a chance to make his peace.

His wife had the same weakness, with this exception: she didn't deny it. One day, standing in the doorway of the rectory, she assured me with happiness that her son was a good boy.

"He never fails to pick me up," she said, "when I'm lying drunk in the hallway, Father. He carries me into the house and puts me to bed." My hope is that God may grant a special blessing to that son.

That father and mother epitomized a common weakness: they were shiftless. They had faith. They were never too far from the Church. But they had no will to set their lives and their economy in order. For example, when the woman told me about the goodness of her son, I felt my heart go out to her. She was wrong, I knew, but I couldn't face that brand of honesty without compassion. In fact, she disarmed me. I didn't know what to say. I could only grasp her hand and hope mightily that He would do what I couldn't.

In one way, I was lucky. I entered the priesthood at a time when the Irish priest was still the administrator of his flock's daily well-being, in addition to their spiritual health. In my time, in my parish, the priests settled all sorts of disputes. Mostly these consisted of arguments between husbands and wives. On many an occasion, the husband and the wife came to the rectory separately, and I told them that, to settle the problem, both must come together, each story must be told in the presence of the other, and that both must agree in advance to follow the advice given.

One of the cases concerned a young woman, who arrived distraught, from another city. She said that she had been keeping company with a young man from St. Michael's, and

83

that he had given her an engagement ring. Now, she learned (and at this point the tears started to flow) that he was married. I sent for the young man and his wife. He was shamed "publicly." He admitted the deception and vowed that he would never "play around" again. I made him apologize to the girl, and to his wife. I told him that he wasn't worthy of either of them. He admitted it. He was badly frightened, and I never had trouble with him again.

Another type of case which frequently came to the door was the jealous wife. She sees her husband talk to another woman, no matter how innocently, and she puts a false interpretation on the conversation. She literally eats her heart out with evil thoughts. She drives herself almost insane. Over a period of thirty years, I found that there was little I could do with a wife of this kind. She's a good woman indeed. But she's wrong. I try always to remember these women in my prayers, because, in the midst of life and happiness, they are sick with suspicion.

Still, the saddest of them all is that of a good woman when she comes to tell you that her husband has left her. In most cases, the woman is healthy, attractive, a good housekeeper, a good mother, a God-fearing woman—in short, the ideal wife for a Catholic man. When they sit in the rectory, fumbling with the clasp on their purses, trying to tell the story and still hold back the tears, your heart sinks. What *can* a priest do? What can he say that will ameliorate this awful thing? Nothing usually except pray. You clasp your hands and you look out the window, and you tell yourself that her life is finished; that, somehow, she is going to have to find a job and support her youngsters, who do not understand, who will never understand. . . .

I don't think that there is a priest anywhere who has not learned that too much mother-in-law breaks up many homes.

Jokes have been told about it, and millions have laughed, but it isn't funny, McGee. It isn't funny at all. What makes it very unfunny is that, in about 90 per cent of the cases, the mother-in-law, responsible for the trouble, is herself a good woman.

Let me tell you a story. The woman I have in mind was a devout person, an indefatigable church worker. She served on any committee for any good cause, and she worked hard at it. She had an attractive daughter who was most exact in the fulfillment of her duties. And the daughter married a good young man with a steady job. Now, instead of setting up by themselves—as Mamma herself had done years before —they decided to live with Mamma. The marriage couldn't have been more than a couple of months old when trouble began. It was Mamma this and Mamma that, and Mamma thinks we ought to do this, and Mamma doesn't want to go to the movies so I'm not going either.

Well, you know what happened. A male is a male. The young man felt, and rightfully so, that he was a boob. That Mary loved her mother more than she did him. So he quit. He walked out. And the ironic thing is that it broke his heart. He loved her. He hoped that she would ask him to come back. But she didn't. After all, there was no gap of love in her life. She still had her mother. Once more, I felt bad, but there was nothing I could do. Divorce was out of the question, so they lived apart.

All this happened a good number of years ago. But God sometimes has mercy on young people when he calls the old to Him. The mother died. And the daughter's grief was enormous. And who do you think consoled her at a time like that? Of course, the young husband. Afterward they went back to living together, and today they are very happy and have a fine family. I just wonder, when those youngsters grow

85

up, will the mamma advise them to get married and live by themselves, or will she plead that she is old and forgotten and wishes they would take her in? Yes, I wonder about a lot of things.

Let me tell you about Mr. and Mrs. Delafield. That isn't the correct name, so no one will be hurt. The Delafields had four lovely children, all arranged in steps and stairs. Neither of the parents was Catholic, but they sent the youngsters to St. Michael's School. Delafield was a big man. He had a chest like a barrel and a neck about the thickness of his jaw. He was as good-natured as he was big. His weakness was liquor, and liquor can be an amiable weakness if, by the drinking, no one but the drinker is hurt. But Delafield, who loved his wife and children with intense passion, had an unhappy faculty for staying on the wagon until a big pay came along. Then he would get drunk and go off on a binge for a week.

His poor wife tried everything. She loved him, and she wouldn't dream of threatening to walk out with the children. But, when he sobered up, he was remorseful and told her that she was too good for him, that he was a no-good bum, and so forth. Finally, she came to me and asked me for instructions. She wanted to be converted. So I sent her to the good sisters, and, in time, she was received into the Church. She seemed to feel that Catholicity offered something, some inner strength, that would help her to bear her troubles. And, of course, it has.

Well, the Delafields lived in a cold-water flat on the third floor of a tenement a few doors away from the church. In the rear, instead of a porch, they had a small fire-escape landing. One morning, while Mrs. Delafield was working, she put the youngest boy out on the first escape for the sun. She was scrubbing and dusting and washing out pants and socks,

86

and every now and then, she called out to the boy. And he would yip his answer, as little boys have done from time immemorial.

She perspired as she worked, and she called out again. And again he emitted the little shriek of happiness that comes only from boys who are devoted to their mothers. And later, she called again. But this time there was no answer. She called again, twice as cheerfully. No answer. Her great heart paused. And she ran to the back window. The little boy was not on the fire escape. Down in the back yard, some men were running. And, on the flagstones, she saw the little suit of clothes, the tiny legs, and the shoes. He was dead before anyone could pick him up.

What it did to that mother, none of us will know. I have seen cases of nervous breakdown, and moral breakdown too. The only thing I can say about poor Mrs. Delafield is that her mind and her heart died at that instant. After the funeral, when Delafield came home, he saw his wife sitting at the kitchen table, a bottle in front of her, humming to herself. The older children stood in the corners of the room, watching, saying nothing. Mr. Delafield begged her to stop. I begged her to stop. We pleaded with her. We reasoned with her. At those times, she wept uncontrollably. The tears staggered down her cheeks, but there was no sound of crying. She wrung her hands, and she promised to try to stop.

But it wasn't in her to stop. Her mind and her heart had died in the instant that her baby had died. And, without a mind and a heart, the soul cannot listen. It is short-circuited. She drank more and more. Then she began to disappear. She would go away for a time, and then she would return. Delafield was the beau ideal at a time like this. He stopped drinking. His sole concern was his wife. No matter how many times she left, no matter how long she was away, no matter what happened while she was away, he always took her back. And not just for the sake of the children, either.

I watched her deterioration as you would watch a building crumble before your eyes. She was picked up by the police and sent to jail. She was picked up again and again. Then she took to disappearing for months at a time. Delafield and I followed every clew to locate her. The last time we caught up with Mrs. Delafield, we had her sentenced to the county hospital in Secaucus.

Three months later, just before school opened, Delafield begged me to get her out. She was sober now. She was a different person. She had been reborn. I helped. The day she came home, he was the happiest man in Jersey City. If a tax had to be paid on happiness, Delafield owed a million dollars the day he escorted her into the house. The next morning she disappeared and hasn't been seen since. She has consorted with the lowest dregs and has given birth to at least two other children by other men.

It was that last bit of news that finished Mr. Delafield. He started to drink again, and abandoned his three children. I placed them in an institution through Catholic Charities.

Mostly, though, the problems of the rectory concern themselves with young married couples who complain that their marriage is doomed. They cannot make a go of it. Usually, one comes in first. If you can get the other half of the bargain to join the party, you're halfway toward a solution. Without ever having been married, a priest usually learns more about marriage than the average married couple. He hears *all* the stories from all sides. My opinion, for whatever it is worth, is that no marriage is completely harmonious. Especially at the start. You can't take two distinct personalities and put them together for life, with their individual ideas about home

88

life and affection and economy and independence, and expect that they are going to "hit it off" at once, and stay happily married forever. Bear in mind that in courtship it is natural for both of them to present only the nice side, the gentler side, to the other person. Before marriage, most couples are congenial and sweet and noble. After marriage we tend to become ourselves. It is this factor, this relaxation of self after the wedding, that breeds most of the trouble. Poor Josie never realized that he likes to eat crackers in bed. And Jimmy, the poor guy, he never stopped to realize that her mother never taught her how to cook.

Both Josie and Jimmy are essentially good persons, but they need a period of adjustment. She must learn to be patient with that crackers-in-bed aspect, while he must learn to encourage her to cook, and to praise her cooking when it is humanly possible without gagging. This period of adjustment sometimes takes a year; I've seen it take as long as four or five before the two began to pull in harness as one unit.

I married a couple a few years back, and at the ceremony I felt a glow of happiness because this was one couple that would never have trouble. They grew up next door to each other. They knew each other as well as it is possible to know another being. And what happened? In six months the bride was before me, in tears. She never realized, she said, what a filthy man he was. Every morning he came to the breakfast table in his pajamas with his hair uncombed. They've since become adjusted. Now both of them come to the breakfast table with unkempt hair.

We had a Polish kid who had been shell-shocked in World War II, and he married one of our Irish colleens. It wasn't too long after the ceremony that she made the pilgrimage to the rectory, and I wondered what could be wrong so soon. I soon found out. When he became angry with her, he dragged her into the bathroom, stuck her head down in the bowl, and flushed the toilet. I thought I had heard everything, but this was a new one. I told her that he was a cad, but I couldn't resist adding that he was one husband who gave his wife plenty of toilet water. I called him in, and he dropped that habit real fast. This couple too has since become adjusted.

Once in a while, as is true everywhere else, we have a couple who did not obey the laws of love. A girl walks in and says she's going to have a baby. She's not married. No court in the land can handle cases like this with the finesse and tact of a priest. Under his guidance, terror is dispelled, anxiety disappears, and crushed hearts and tortured minds are mended. There are few cases in which the priest stands closer to the true mercy of Christ than this one.

His heart must go out to the girl. It has to. The boy has suffered no ill effects, and quite often he feels no real sense of shame. But the girl—that's different. Soon the whole neighborhood will know her story. Soon she will be whispered about behind the hands of the mothers hanging wash in the back yard. Soon the boys of the neighborhood will know, and they will laugh and make indecent suggestions. Soon, worst of all, her father will know, and his bitter invective will be heaped upon her and her mother.

It is at this time that the priest can repair damage; can straighten out two lives; can talk a decent boy into doing the right thing; can cover up for the girl and ease her heartache; can work miracles of reason and out of despair bring hope and life and a future.

Another rectory problem is the matter of baptismal certificates. All churches have this trouble, and St. Michael's had more than its share. Some of them don't know when they were born, so the priest checks the records within five years either way of what he supposes the parishioner's age to be.

Another one isn't quite sure of the correct spelling: he spells it "Coughran," but his mother always insisted it was "Coughlin," but his father was just as certain that it should be "Coughlan." And then there's the lady who gets impatient and taps her foot while the priest hunts for her baptismal record, and, after a while, she laughs and covers her mouth with her hand and says, "Oh, stupid, stupid me. I just remembered. My father and mother were married here, but I was christened in St. Bridget's. I'm so sorry, Father."

During the war we had a lot of parishioners, more women then men, who wanted us to alter the records. They could get a job in such and such a war plant, but they were only taking on girls up to age thirty-five, and right now, Father, I'm fifty-five, but all you have to do is change the five to a three. When we refused, we received glares that would melt a statue down to putty.

There was a well-known character in St. Michael's, the Lord be good to him, and his name was Tom Boyle. If Tom had had a high-school and college education, he would have become a great political leader. He became the deputy ward leader in the Horseshoe, under John V. Kenny, and subsequently he became a member of the Hudson County Board of Freeholders. Tom was forever helping somebody, and one of the things he was called upon to do was to get baptismal certificates that could be custom-made.

Tom was sitting in the waiting room of St. Peter's Rectory one day, and he spotted a pad of blank baptismal records. This was exactly what Tom needed, so he appropriated the whole pad. Soon there appeared a flock of certificates from St. Peter's Church with the signature of a priest at the bottom. Tom used these spurious things to get jobs for people, and I suppose he did a lot of good with them. But he made a bad mistake. When he went to confession, he went to the same priest from whom he had stolen the pad, and, it being a sin to steal, he confessed it. When the priest cut loose on Tom, the explosions could be heard all the way to the next parish.

But Tom had so many virtues that if he had robbed a bank I think that half the parish would have gone his bail, and the other half would have prayed for his acquittal. He never stopped doing favors. When the head of a family lost his job, Tom Boyle's unremitting efforts went toward finding the man a new one. When a widow lacked rent money, Tom got it for her. In a coal or an oil crisis, Boyle was the one man to be seen standing on a running board, delivering the scarce material in person. Once, when we had a church election, I asked him if he could get me a couple of small boxes with holes in the top. He returned with three full-size election ballot boxes. When the election was done, I tried to return them to Tom. He just shrugged and smiled. They are still in the church basement.

As is the case with most of us, Tom's greatest enemy was himself. He was a periodical drinker. For long periods he would remain sober and have no inclination to touch the stuff. Then, without warning, he'd go off and he'd drink until he couldn't stand, and when he could no longer sit he'd lie down and drink. It may be that Tom's gentle spirit could stand only so much of human misery without breaking down. He seldom saw happiness; people who were happy didn't need Tom Boyle. Everybody who sought him had a problem, and every problem was of the most desperate urgency. It could be that the woes of man piled up inside him, higher and higher, until he could accept no more. Then he drank. He drank to forget; to wash the accumulated sorrows of his people from the face of his heart.

I was called one morning. The caller said to please hurry;

92

Tom Boyle had been found dead in bed. He was gone before I arrived, but I prayed fervently that God would bear in mind all the fine things Tom had done for others. His funeral was the biggest I've ever seen at St. Michael's, and I've seen some big ones. Unfortunately, one of the local newspapers, in its lengthy obituary, referred to Tom's weakness and, by implication, made it appear that excessive drinking was one of the vices of the Horseshoe. I bridled sufficiently to phone the editor, reminding him of the adage, "De mortuis nil nisi bonum" (Speak only good of the dead) and I also reminded him of John Hays' "Jim Bludso."

> *Wall, no! I can't tell whar he lives,*
> *Because he don't live, you see;*
> *Leastways, he's got out of the habit*
> *Of livin' like you and me. . . .*

> *He were n't no saint,—but at jedgement*
> *I'd run my chance with Jim,*
> *'Longside of some pious gentleman*
> *That wouldn't shook hands with him.*
> *He seen his duty, a dead-sure thing,—*
> *And went for it there and then,*
> *And Christ ain't a going to be too hard*
> *On a man that died for men.*

No matter how patient and saintly a priest may be, you can arouse him by bringing up the matter of sick calls. In no field of church work is the average priest more abused than in this. At St. Michael's, no matter how we urged the parish to please, please phone us during the day when a member of the family was ill, they seemed to have a penchant for 2 A.M., 3 A.M., and 4 A.M. I do not mean that all night calls can be avoided. When sickness comes suddenly and violently,

93

it is no respecter of the clock. No, I refer to cases in which the victim has been ill for days or weeks, and has been sinking slowly toward the comatose quiet of death. No call comes to the rectory until that person is practically standing in the valley of darkness.

Then the call comes. And it's always in a roaring hurry. They plead for quick action; they sob; they beg; and the priest, half asleep, assures the person that he will dress immediately and be right over. I have done it many a night when the snow swirled in great maelstroms out of the night sky, walking fast, slipping and sliding, and hoping that, if the family didn't give me enough time, God would. At a time like that, it seems almost uncanny that the dying person *had* to live on the top floor of a tenement.

Much has been written about the apostolate of the sick. It is greater, by far, than the apostolate of preaching, and— take it from one who has spent thirty-five years making sick calls—the priest himself rises or falls in the estimation of his people at that precise moment. He may preach a poor sermon, or stutter, or lack a sense of humor, but when tragedy strikes the home, the people think nothing of a brilliant canonist or an astute theologian. They want help, and they want it quickly. The doctor has told them that the patient is dying, and now there is nothing left but the final great hope of eternity. When the priest arrives, the women will weep and the men will fall to their knees, but there is a sense of relief in the house. They watch him go into the bedroom, and they remain outside. They know that *something . . . is . . . being . . . done.*

That's all it is. Where the doctor failed, the priest succeeds. If only you could get them to understand that Extreme Unction is not the mark of death, to be used only when the death rattle is plain for all to hear. If only you could get them to understand that the Host brings comfort and a feeling of well-being to the sick person; it arms him against anything the Devil can do, and the sick person realizes it. But no. They're all afraid to call the priest ahead of time. "If a priest walked in here right now, it would kill Mom for sure." "She feels a little better today, and if we called Father it would push her over the edge." Nothing is farther from the truth.

I have administered the last rites to persons who were just getting into heaven under the line. After a lifetime of sin and of having tasted every pleasure and vice, God gives them a chance, a chance to die in a state of grace. If ever there was proof of His Infinite Mercy, this is it. The most unworthy of people, the people who defiled His name all their lives, are given the opportunity of walking, head high, up to the gates of heaven beside the good people who remembered Him and loved Him all their lives.

One morning I was summoned to the bedside of an attractive blonde. Her body was as beautiful as her soul was ugly. Everyone in the parish knew that she had taken various lovers. She had taken them, and dropped them without pity when she tired. But the last one had beaten her to the romantic punch. He had dropped her. And her pride couldn't stand it, so, at the moment I entered the room, she was dying from an overdose of sleeping pills.

She too was given the rare chance. When I left her, I felt happy that she was now in a state of preparedness to meet her Maker. And I felt sorry too; sorry that anyone with the gifts God gave her could not have made better use of them in life. Apparently her hour had not yet come. God gave her another chance and she recovered. A short time later she moved from the parish, and I've never seen her again. But many a time I've wondered if she heeded the warning. Had she returned to the Church, penitent over the past, and determined to rebuild her life along His way? Or has she reverted to type? I do not know. I wish I did.

She had several sisters, this girl, and they too were attractive. But every one of them, sooner or later, sank to the lowest dregs of society. The husband of one was arrested as a gangster. When he went to jail, his loving wife found another man. The children of these women were many, and they were slovenly and careless and would smile up at you in great innocence, while at the same time stealing the crucifix off its chain. The children grew up as unfitted for life and responsibility as the mothers. Even the Irish have those of whom they are ashamed.

The non-emergency sick calls are the ones that bring the greatest happiness to the priest. These are the regulars, the chronically ill, the aged, and the infirm. They are the most cheerful people in the world. They radiate such gratitude when the priest comes to visit them, once a month, that he is humbled anew by it. The little girl with the twisted legs, living in the third floor rear, is scrubbed and smiling when you walk in. You feel your throat constrict, and the words issue from your mouth like growls. This little girl will never walk again, but she looks up at you almost with adoration, as though you were doing the greatest favor in the world for her—as indeed you are.

God must do something special to the souls of these people, to make them feel so happy. The man with the failing heart looks gray of skin, and he struggles to breathe; but the moment he sees you his eyes sparkle, his face beams, and he reaches out a friendly hand to you. The old lady in the wheel chair saves her best bed jacket for this one day of Communion. Hers is a wasting disease, and she grows smaller and weaker with each visit. But her main concern is you, the priest. She is sure that you are doing too much and you are working too hard, and she always admonishes you to take it easy, that God's vineyard is immense and that no one worker can carry all the grapes.

There are many of them in my parish. Many of them. They are of all sizes and ages and dispositions, but on the morning of your visit they look whole again, happy again, and you bring to them the One Great Friend who will never desert them. They know that. And you know that they know it.

Even a gambler can have a good heart. I knew one, at least. In the middle of St. Michael's, for a number of years, stood the biggest gambling center in the East. The business it did was beyond my comprehension, but I know that millions of dollars passed in and out of this place. It was run by two men: Charles Good and Gene Sullivan.

In spite of the way Gene made his money, he kept up his church duties. How he reconciled the two I'll never know. Maybe his philosophy was that, when one of his customers bet on a horse, the customer selected the horse and all Gene did was to bet that the man was wrong, thereby proving that gambling doesn't pay. But, whatever his reasoning, Gene had heart trouble, and he had it bad. On two occasions he collapsed in the doorway of a cigar store at the corner of Grove Street and Pavonia Avenue (a famous meeting place once called Neilan's Park House), and each time I absolved him conditionally and each time he recovered.

The third time I was called was, to say the least, dramatic. The call led me to the inner sanctum of the gambling parlor itself. It was on the second floor of a multiple dwelling right over Sullivan's Saloon. There were two rooms, and in the first one was a long table with many telephones and a loudspeaker which announced which race was on, and how the nags were running. At the end of this table Gene Sullivan was slumped, unconscious, in a chair.

I did not want to administer the last rites in the blaring atmosphere of a horse parlor; so with the assistance of a couple of bookies whose phones, at the moment, were silent, we got Gene into the second room, which was quiet. I anointed him, and this time, before I left, he had returned to consciousness. I told him that he belonged in St. Francis Hospital and had better get there quick. Gene agreed, and the ambulance took him away. He improved for a while. Then he weakened and died.

When his will was read, I was astounded. I found that I had been named executor of his estate. He made all sorts of bequests—and a good one to St. Michael's Church—but, even though millions of dollars had passed through his hands, Gene Sullivan died broke. His debts were greater than his assets, and he himself turned out to be the best proof that gambling does not pay. His partner, Charlie Good, dropped dead on a golf course. They were both affable, kind, and charitable. The only testimony I can render in their favor is negative: no wife or daughter ever came to the rectory to complain about husbands or fathers squandering their money with Good or Sullivan.

There were two occasions when I was called to attend men who had committed suicide. One occurred at seven in the morning in Hamilton Park, across the street from the rectory. I was in the vestibule of the church, and I ran across the street when I heard the shot. Others were running too. There, inside the fence and under the big evergreen bushes, lay a man of Polish extraction. I absolved and anointed him conditionally, which safeguards the sacraments and is the proper procedure in these cases. The man was unknown to me.

98

Perhaps I had better explain this. Conditional Absolution is given in the case of a person who is found unconscious or in a coma, or who has died suddenly. According to most theologians, life stays on in the body for several hours after apparent death. The form generally used is, *"Si capax es."* (If you are capable, I absolve you from your sins, in the name of the Father, the Son, and the Holy Ghost. Amen.) This safeguards the squandering of the sacrament, and prevents it from being invalid. Also, one of the conditions of conditional Absolution is that the person so favored will on recovery go at once to the sacraments and make a full confession. Of course, if the person does not recover, he cannot make good the condition. Always, however, in cases of necessity, as in shipwreck and street accidents, however great the distance, conditional Absolution may be given.

The second suicide occurred at 7:30 A.M. in the home of one of my parishioners. He was an Irishman, living with a good wife and two fine daughters. What made him do it no one knows. But, at that hour of the morning, he walked into the bedroom, stuck the barrel of a gun down his throat, and pulled the trigger. When I arrived, there was no face, only blood. I administered conditional Absolution and did my best to calm his wife and children. They were in hysterics. I tried to find a reason for the suicide, but there was no history of unhappiness, no great problems, no bickering. I could only conclude that the man, for the moment, had lost his mind. He was given all the honors of the Church—Mass, blessing, and the privilege of resting in consecrated ground.

All cases of suicide must be referred to the chancery office for an official decision, but, in the absence of evidence to the contrary, it is assumed that a man who kills himself is not a creature of reason at the moment of the act. Thus, if it is agreed that he or she was insane at the time, proper

99

Catholic burial is indicated. On the other hand, it is recognized that the deliberate—sane—destruction of self is possible, and, in such cases, it is clearly a mortal sin, and Mass and ecclesiastical burial must be refused.

There are other things in St. Michael's Parish besides tenements and brownstones. At the foot of Twelfth Street and the Hudson River are the President Line piers and, not far away, the Erie tube station, the Erie Railroad terminal, a large packing plant owned by Swift & Company, and several other large industrial areas where accidents can, and do, occur. We have had men fall from a height and be killed; a railroad man slips between cars and his legs are amputated, and he must be attended to out on the tracks. Another man slipped and was buried beneath tons of coal. When his friends dug him out, he was dead, the coal dust glinting brightly on his still-open eyes. There are explosions and great fires. St. Michael's is not a dull parish.

Some of the homes we must visit are filthy beyond understanding. Once inside, it is difficult to breathe. The dirt is shoe-leather high. The people who live in such places must be so accustomed to it that they no longer see it. But when you come in out of bright yellow sunshine and heady air into darkness and dirt and an odor of mildewed decomposition, you notice it plainly.

A case in point was Martin Beattie. He lived with two old spinster sisters, and he had been blind for two decades. He was in the house most of the time, and when he wasn't he was in the back yard. There, in his darkness, he chopped wood for the kitchen stove. He never went anywhere else, and no one ever thought of taking him anywhere else.

Once a year I brought Communion to him. And at each annual visit I'd suggest that old Martin Beattie permit me to call upon him once a month. And each year I received the same answer, "Father, I wouldn't be puttin' you to all that trouble. For the likes of me once a year is enough."

I never heard Martin Beattie complain. He lived in disgusting filth, but when he wasn't chopping wood he sat in his rocker in silence, rosary in hand, thinking whatever thoughts the blind think, now and then remembering what it was like to be able to see. In my estimation he was one of the saints of everyday life, as good and as uncomplaining as a martyr.

When he became so ill that he had to be taken to St. Francis Hospital, he arrived covered with bug powder. The lice must have been with him many years, and he had endured it in silent anguish. When I administered the last rites of Holy Mother Church, I felt inferior. I felt that I was in the presence of great sanctity. He had endured without complaint, and yet he had been helpless to help himself.

And then as I watched him sinking slowly, never asking for a drop of water, never complaining of his pain, I suddenly thought that right here, this Martin Beattie, had all the riches and the honor of the truly distinguished men of the earth; that one becomes great not through the applause of others, but by the growth of sanctifying grace in one's soul. This man, perhaps more than any of us, had truly trod the Way of the Cross, and he therefore was greater than any of us. I hope that he will pray for me.

There were other fine people in St. Michael's, many of them no longer with us. Unless you lived there, you never saw the likes of Mary Bradley. She was a big woman in every way, physically, mentally, spiritually. She was there when I first arrived from the seminary, and she bore the same affection for me that she had for her son Jack. If ever I had a friend in the parish, it was Mrs. Mary Bradley. And if anyone ever said a word against me in the presence of Mary Bradley, she would swing her old shillelagh and demolish the offender and his whole family unto the third cousins once removed.

Mrs. Bradley was the president of the Rosary Society and the undisputed leader of the women of the parish. Thinking back now, especially between the years 1930 to 1947, I can't recall a church activity that she didn't lead. She had only two interests: her fine family and her church. That encompassed her entire horizon. The work she did was as gigantic as she. And once she started on a project, it was considered wise for all parishioners, and priests too, to step aside because she leveled everything in her way.

Finally her heart gave way, and she was confined to bed. But when she felt a little bit better, she climbed a flight of stairs. This was against doctor's orders and against the wishes of everyone who loved her. But unless you knew Mary Bradley, you wouldn't understand how impossible it was to forbid her to do anything. She climbed the stairs, and in a few minutes she was back in bed, never to rise again.

I make it a practice to restrain my emotions, but when Mary Bradley died, I was miserable. Had I been truly her son, I could not have felt worse. I don't effuse, but in *Parish Interests* I wrote a long effusion about her, and I concluded by writing:

"We accorded to her in death the honors usually associated only with those in high station. But no one knows better than ourselves how well they were deserved and the lofty eminence that was hers in the eyes of her Creator whom she loved and served so well. She was a wonderful woman and it will be a long time, if ever, that we find the like of her again. May her great soul rest in peace."

6

YOU MAY recall that I told you that one of my first assignments was the altar boys. The darlings, I felt like murdering them half the time. If they were good, it was when they were sound asleep. Even then, I wouldn't be too sure. I was amused, years later, reading a piece written by Father Hugh Calkins. He had worked on the film story of the Mass, a picture called *The Eternal Gift,* and he wrote about the behind-the-scenes stories in the studio. "Still there were laughs," he wrote. "Never a dull moment with our altar boys—the dirty-faced angels!" Between takes, these fine Catholic boys dealt a sizzling hot-foot to relaxing actors, and they broke the technical crew shooting dice and playing pinochle.

The boys set up a record phone bill too. "The cassocked little saints were dating girls all over town with calls like: 'This is Tyrone O'Keefe. What's cooking tonight?' "

The altar boys of the Horseshoe were always said to be hard-boiled, but I think that there are tricks which haven't occurred to our kids. Still, it seems to me that the boys of St. Michael's had far more vitality, and were up to more tricks, than when I was an altar boy.

It was my job to teach the ceremonies to them and to give them the fundamentals of serving Mass, vespers, and benediction. They had to be able to serve or to sing, and if they could do both, so much the better. The organist, Dr. Julia Harney, had charge of the singing. She was born and raised in St. Michael's, and had the unique distinction of having lived through the tenures of all five pastors.

On Friday afternoons, without fail, Dr. Harney conducted rehearsals around the corner in the old school hall. As she sat at the piano, her back was to the boys. My job was to be there and enforce discipline. One afternoon I showed up a few minutes late, and I saw at once that matters were coming to a boil. Little John Hawkes was standing directly behind Dr. Harney, his two thumbs stuck in his ears and his fingers wiggling at a great rate. It did look funny, and it was difficult to suppress a smile. However, duty is duty, and I walked across the room and picked John up and suspended him directly over my head. I carried him down to the three steps in the rear of the hall and gave John the heave-ho. Then I returned to the rest of the sugar plums and said, "Well, who's next?"

There was no more trouble that day. A long time later, John Hawkes became a flying officer in the Navy, and was selected to accompany Admiral Byrd on his last polar expedition. But his first flying lesson he received from me.

In those days St. Michael's was still old-fashioned enough to have vespers every Sunday evening. No one else did, as far as I recall, but the Old Man said "carry on," and carry on we did. Usually we had about sixty altar boys, sometimes more, sometimes less. They came and went, sometimes voluntarily but more often involuntarily.

Among them, at one time, were Frank Sheridan, Ogden Dates, and Gerald Moore. These three were always on their toes, punctual, reverent, and respectful. All three are priests today. Frank became assistant pastor of St. Mary's in Rahway, New Jersey, Ogden became a Jesuit theologian and dean of philosophy at Woodstock College, Maryland, and Gerald became a Passionist Father and vice-rector of St. Michael's Monastery in Union City, New Jersey.

On one particular Sunday, under the leadership of "Smock" O'Keefe, it was decided that it was time to show that runt McWilliams something. Too long had they been pushed around, their rights abrogated, their privileges revoked. Who did he think he was, that sawed-off, hammered-down little half pint, that apology for a circus midget? They laid their plans well. At vespers, they filed out into their seats, located at the time beyond the altar rail. In surplice, cope, and stole, I brought up the rear of the procession, genuflected before the main altar, and knelt down for the Pater and Ave.

Returning to the bench, I remained standing to intone the opening *"Deus in adjutorium"* and the *"Dixit Dominus"* of the first psalm of Sunday vespers. Then I sat, expecting to hear from the stalls the response of the first verse, *"Domino meo sede a dextris meis."* But there was no echo that night. Surprised and choking, I took up the second verse, *"Donec ponam inimicos tuos,"* and waited to hear their *"Scabellum pedum tuorum."* Not a word came back to me. Not a sound from anywhere. Now I began to realize that the boys were giving me the business, yet I wasn't altogether sure.

And so I began intoning the first part of the third verse, *"Virgum virtutis tuae emittet Dominus ex Sion";* and I waited to hear *"Dominare in medio inimicorum tuorum."* Silence again. It was then that I realized that the strike of the altar boys was on. To say that I was chagrined is to understate it. I was boiling. But there was nothing I could do about it. It had to continue as a one-man show, to the enjoyment of the cherubs in the box seats. I caught the eye of Dr. Harney, in the choir loft. Even though she realized what was going on—she too was stuck, and had to continue to play the organ. The faces of the people in the church looked shocked.

The break came after the hymn *"Lucis Creator Optime"* had been sung and I intoned the *Magnificat.* Sheridan and Dates and Moore, unwilling radicals in the strike, and at the risk of being called scabs, took up the beautiful canticle of Our Lady and carried it through to the end. A few others began to feel frightened, and they joined in the concluding responses and, when I heard the final "Amen" after the last versicle, *"Fidelium animae per misericordiam Dei requiescat in pace,"* I knew that the worst was over. Benediction of the Blessed Sacrament closed the services, and also the short triumph of the dead-end kids.

We returned to the priest's sacristy, and after bowing to the crucifix and to them, I said, "And all of you boys will now wait in the other sacristy until I tell you to go." Before they even arrived at the sacristy, I was on top of them, having hastily discarded my vestments.

I knew that tact was of no use. These youngsters were from the water front, and they had hearts of steel. So I stood among them, and demanded in the tone of doom whether "Smock" O'Keefe was the ringleader. After some hesitation, a few of the boys nodded.

"O'Keefe," I roared, "come here."

He came up to me, and I let him have it—wham! Then I went down the line and between the rows, swinging right and left. I didn't stop flailing until the last culprit had been punished. The strike of the altar boys was over. They left the church with their heads down. That was the last of the strikes, and there has never been one since. It was McWilliams who won that strike, the sawed-off, hammered-down, etc.

Despite the strike, the boys we had represented the best in the parish. They had the makings of excellent Catholics and Americans. Now and then, it was necessary to pin their ears back, and when it was coming, they got it from me. Once in a while, a parent would object, but most of them were solidly behind me and gave me the authority to make men out of their boys.

Many a man of today was my boy yesterday, and many of the best of them were whacked and thumped when it was necessary. Lawyers, business executives, doctors—all are so dignified, almost regal, today. But, in my mind's eye, I can still see the freckles, the unkempt hair, the patched pants, the holes in the stockings, and the stunned shock when I caught them doing something wrong. Others, besides the three I mentioned, who have become priests, are Father Thomas Reardon, navy chaplain of Guadalcanal fame, and his two cousins, Edward and Bill Looney. The former is director of the New Jersey Boys' Town at Arlington, and the latter is pastor of St. Patrick's Church at Chatham, New Jersey. Then there was Timothy Holland, a great little bundle from the Horseshoe, who is now a member of the Josephite Order; Thomas Finn, Jr., who now has a wife and five children and is superintendent of the Hudson County Tubercular Hospital; Michael Burke is now a captain in the Jersey City Fire Department; my old friend Smock O'Keefe has achieved great success in the business world, and today we are real friends. When I recall to them the good old days, they light up briefly with a roguish smile, and then they straighten their faces and shake their heads sadly.

But when I think back on those days, I do not shake my head sadly. Sometimes, in the silence of my study, I laugh and laugh, and, if any of my young curates pass by, I'm sure that they think that the old man has blown all his fuses; but, to me, they were really great days, no matter how angry I may have been at the time. Why, I can go into a fit of laughing right now when I think of a certain night, very long ago, when all the altar boys showed up for services except one. That one was a bit late. When he came in, he had a big bag full of horse manure. (The boys called it Irish turkey.) And he went around to the coats of each of the boys, and each one got its quota.

Then, unobtrusively, our hero donned his cassock and left the sacristy and joined the others. I often wonder about his pious, holy thoughts as he joined the others in the sacred hymns. I'm sure that his little mind was not on the hymns. When the services were over, he joined the others in hurrying to doff the cassocks and surplices, and he just watched and watched and watched. Then his patience was rewarded. The first boy had put his coat on, felt something heavy in one pocket, and stuck his hand into moist gold. The boy yelled. Then another boy did the same. And another. They held the wet hands in front of them, fingers spread apart, and the odor was unbearable. Whoever the horse had been, he was in prime health. The bedlam was riotous. The sister moderator in charge kept her head and thus prevented hand grenades from being thrown all over the place. By the time I skidded into the room, order had been restored.

My first question (it seems to be an eternal one) was, "Who did it?"

There was no answer. No one knew anything, and the

108

perpetrator was not going to confess his guilt. In situations of this kind, the priest must win. If he loses but one battle, the boys will never stop trying to defeat him again. The next day was Saturday.

"All right," I said. "We'll have a special meeting tomorrow at 9 A.M. I want everybody to be here, and no excuses. In fact, anyone who isn't here will be presumed to have had a hand in this thing."

When they arrived the next day, I called the roll, and all hands were present. I explained with kindness, I thought, that this was the last chance for the guilty boy or boys to confess. Again, silence. So I marched them over to the laboratory of the school, put them inside, turned the key, and said that I would return every hour on the hour until the guilty confessed. I kept this up for three hours, and it looked as if I were in for a difficult time of it. Then Paul Harnett stepped forward sheepishly and admitted that he, and he alone, had stuffed the Irish turkey in the pockets.

I suspended him immediately. The others were permitted to go home. But Paul Harnett will never know the strength of character I displayed when I kept the bubbling laughter inside me, and maintained a stern face. Paul became a fine citizen, respected everywhere, and so did his brothers, John and Frank. Paul later passed on.

In all my years at St. Michael's, we've had only two thefts by altar boys. The first occurred on a Sunday morning when twenty-one dollars was missing from the collection basket. Only the ushers and the altar boys knew that, between Masses, the change was kept in a certain closet. Stealing is not a prank. It doesn't fall into a category with the other things I've discussed. It's important because it represents a defect of character. And, quite often, a permanent defect. And yet I was not going to put myself into the awkward position of accusing all the boys, or of locking them up until one confessed. No, this required different handling.

I kept quiet, and results came quickly. The sister sacristan came to me and said that she was sure that the thief was in her school class. She said that he was an altar boy, and that she despaired of him because he was repeatedly guilty of lying and cheating, and that he was thoroughly dishonest. She said that if I pressed him hard enough he'd confess.

Frankly, I wasn't sure. You can press a boy too hard, and he'll confess to anything. Suddenly, I knew the answer. I called the boy, and I accused him of the theft. He sat in my office and turned the most innocent eyes on me that I've ever seen. I pressed a little harder. Then I pulled my trump from the deck.

"Listen," I said, "you did it and you know you did it. Now, I'll tell you what I'm going to do." I pulled out my watch. "I'll give you ten minutes to go home and get that money— all of it—and be back her   When ten minutes have expired, I'm phoning the police, a   ll put you away in a reformatory for a while. Let's s   at will do you any good."

The boy took off like   fighter. In four minutes, he was back with the money. A   it. I knew the circumstances of his people, and I knew   t would have been impossible for him to get that much   y from his parents, if he were not guilty and merely fri   ed.

He supplied his own s   ce. "Please," he whimpered, "don't tell my father. He   l me."

I threw him out of the g   of altar boys, but I permitted him to worry about whether   u tell his dad or not. Of course I did not tell the man anything, believing that a youngster needs more than one chance to make good. It turned out to be one of the biggest mistakes I ever made.

The boy lived over a drugstore, and the druggist com-

plained to the father that the kid had stolen seventy dollars.
The father came to me bristling with indignation.

"Now how do you like that?" he yelled, red-faced and
helpless. "What should I do, Father, about that druggist?"

There was no easy way of telling that man the truth. So
I shot it to him bluntly. "I'm sorry to say this," I said, "but
I think you may find that the druggist is right." I told him
about the church theft, and of how his son had admitted his
guilt. I never saw a man break down so swiftly. He wept uncontrollably. He was a hard-working laboring man, and as
he wept he tried to tell me what he had done to make a decent
home for his wife and his children, and of how he had even
worked overtime to get in enough money for clothes and the
other things the children needed. He felt now that, somewhere along the line, he had failed.

We investigated the druggist's charge. The first thing discovered was that the boy in question had, only the day pre-
viously, donated fifteen dollars to the Association of the
Holy Childhood, a children's organization which gathers
money for the missions. When he made his donation, the
sister asked him how he was able to make such a large contribution. He turned the innocent eyes on her and said that
he had had a birthday, and the fifteen dollars was part of the
gifts from relatives. The money was turned back to the druggist.

The boy never made good. When he grew up, he was a
hoodlum. He was in trouble with the police most of the time.
A few years ago he moved away, and I have lost track of him.
I don't know what effect all this had on his mother, but I
know he broke his father's heart.

The other case concerned three dollars. Again a sister of
the school tipped me off, and again it was an altar boy. He
confessed, and I told him that I would accept repayment at

the rate of fifty cents a week. This boy was the very soul of penitence. He was truly sorry that he had succumbed to temptation, and felt worse over his own shame at being caught. It took all his spending money through six weeks of a fine summer to repay the money, but repay it he did.

Worst of all, I found out, was the suspension from the altar. Long after he had paid back the three dollars, he would call at the rectory, hat in hand, and ask if he could be reinstated. Perhaps it was harsh on my part, but he was never reinstated. He kept calling at the rectory for at least a year, then he stopped coming. Today he is a father, a good and righteous man, and a credit to his community.

You just never know, do you?

Among other duties—I'll bet you never realized how many there are—is the taking of the census. Once a year we went from house to house, from floor to floor, from door to door, finding out how many people were Catholics, the state of their religious life, their ages and dispositions. Now, it is true that the confessional will give a priest a revealing insight into the internal forum of his flock, but I maintain that there is nothing that will give you a more candid look at man in the external forum than the census. When it is finished each year, the pastor and his priests have a detailed knowledge of the number, but more especially the kind, of people living within the confines of the parish.

It is impossible for a priest to become acquainted with the many and varying problems of the people of his parish unless he can meet each of them face to face. The census is tiring— wearying is a better word. To finish it successfully requires patience and perseverance. Also, the priest must be prepared to withstand humiliation. And each day as you finish a few more houses, or, if you're lucky, a block of them, you return to the rectory beaten and frustrated. You cannot understand how so many Roman Catholics can live almost within the shadow of the crucifix and still remain so indifferent to Christ. You meet complete callousness to sin face to face, and it stares at you shamelessly. Reading about evil, or even considering it theologically, is a whale of a lot different from seeing it.

It's an experience that shook me to my heels. I returned at night to sit in my room and wonder whether I had ever done any good at all. If I had, why was there so much bad within the confines of St. Michael's Parish? Why was it that I didn't realize it until I made the annual canvass? Why did I stand at the top step of the church stairway on Sunday mornings, glorying in the multitudes who left one Mass as many hundreds of other were threading their way through the crowd to attend the next? Why did that make me feel good, when I should have known that there were many hundreds of others who should have been in those crowds, and who weren't?

Was I too smug? Perhaps. Frankly, I didn't know. But this I do know: no poor alcoholic ever trembled more than I. Each night I went through the same dizzying experience, and each night, after reflection, I determined that, even if I persuaded only one of these persons to return to God, I would be that much ahead of the game. I had to adopt a philosophy, or despair would have perched on my shoulder. At one of the early censuses, the words of the economist Devas gave me tremendous comfort, and you may find, as I did, that the more you read this passage, the more you will find new and hidden meanings.

Virtue and sanctity are in great measure secret gifts known only to God and good angels. Evil is uppermost, but everywhere underlined by good. We hear the drunken clamor of the streets, but not the silent worshipers in the watches of the night; we hear the loud iniquity of the prime of life, not the silent change in sickness and old age. We see the rough exterior, the coarse violence, the brutal ungodliness of whole quarters of our great cities, not the compassion and generosity, not the courage and chivalry, not the instinct of prayer concealed all the while below the surface. If we make the search we shall find out daily how harshness in these dark regions avails nothing, while sympathy wins the hearts. There must be a heart then to win. Truly all men are better than they seem and their actions worse than their hearts. But the physicians of our souls are capable of forming a better judgment than the physicians of our bodies, because they look at both good and evil. They see how evil is made the occasion of good, as it were its counterpart and correlative. They read the unwritten record of unexhausted patience, of continuous self-sacrifice, of repentant tears; to whom ill-doers are transmuted into the material for the triumph of grace and appear the yet ungarnered harvest of the Passion and the Cross.

The actual mechanics for taking the census are simple. In general, in the Archdiocese of Newark, it consists of a specially printed card on the top of which is the family name and address. Below are the father's first name, the wife's, and the names of the various children, also the names of any other persons living with the family. Opposite each name are little squares for the age, baptism, First Communion, confirmation, attendance at Mass, performance of Easter duty, school attended, place of work, and membership in any church societies. On the back of the cards there is room for memoranda by the priest.

When the census is properly completed, these cards represent a good picture of the parish, and a thumbnail sketch of everyone in it. From these cards the priest knows his parish thoroughly, and he knows which families require his special attention. Enough follow-up work is uncovered annually to keep a group of priests busy for months.

The day before the start of the census an announcement is made at all Masses on the Sunday preceding. We do not ask everyone to stay home and wait for the priest, because the census will not be completed in one day. We announce that the priest will be visiting on certain streets tomorrow and will persons residing on those streets please see that someone is home. Other streets are announced for other days.

The great majority of families in our parish are delighted to see the priest. Mamma and the children spend hours scrubbing and mopping and dusting and ironing. The house must look its best, and when the priest knocks on the door it is flung open, and he sees shining, smiling faces. Not only is he welcomed—if I partook of every cup of tea offered, my eyes would now be slanted—but he often has difficulty making a graceful exit. It is respect and affection which prevents us from maintaining our schedule.

Of course there are others who do not want to see the priest and who will not answer the door. You walk upstairs slowly, and you hear animated conversation. When you knock, the conversation within dies. There is no answer. No one is home to you. You wait, and you knock again. You know that there are people inside, and you are made to feel like a leprous beggar. Your impulse is to turn the knob and walk in. Usually you do no such thing. You walk back downstairs, and as you pass in front of the house you look up at the windows. A curtain is hurriedly dropped. They didn't want you.

As you know, St. Michael's is not an easy parish to cover. The tenements rise four and five stories, many of them old, creaky places with the rancid odor of forgotten cooking in the halls. Reaching the top floor is akin to climbing the Washington Monument. When you repeat this operation enough times in one day, you are barely able to walk the four stone steps up into the rectory.

The number of families a priest can cover depends very much upon the amount of time he devotes to it, the quickness of the priest himself in getting questions answered, and how long a family keeps him for a recitation of the domestic woes. In my younger days I was amazed at the speed with which Fathers Barrett and Ratigan got around; but they were veterans at census taking, and they knew the ropes so well that I could not hope to compete with them. If they got an early start, and kept at it all day, they would sometimes cover forty or fifty families apiece. As you entered each home, you blessed it: "Peace be unto this house and all who dwell therein."

One of the funniest things that happened—and there were many—was the time a man was seen carrying a door on his back, heading for the rectory. A few minutes later, he pushed the bell and the woman who answered the door looked as though now she had seen everything. The man wanted to see the pastor, so "himself" was called. When the Monsignor walked into the office, even his renowned aplomb was knocked for a loop when he saw a man sitting there with a door.

"It's not doors, now, you're selling," the Monsignor said, "for if it is I'm sorry to tell you that we have all the doors we can use."

The man was grim-lipped. "Your reverence, and beggin' your pardon, Father McElhone was at me flat today takin' the census, and when none answered his knock he put his shoulder to the door and down it came hinges and all. Sure

116

I knew nobody would believe me, so I brought the door along to show you. Now right is right and wrong is wrong, and it's a wonderful thing to take up the census, your reverence. But who in his right mind ever heard of a priest takin' the census and the door at the same time?

"It's no fault I'm after findin' with Father McElhone, as fine a man as ever drew breath of life. He's a grand priest, God bless him, but as I was sayin', your reverence, we have to draw the line somewhere. Now I know you like to know what's goin' on in the parish, and perhaps a word from you to the good father himself might not be out of order."

The Monsignor thanked him for coming over, and for bringing the proof with him. He further assured the man that he would have a little talk with Father McElhone and persuade him to curb his zeal and to proceed with prudence in the future. This made the Irishman feel better, and he left, after much bowing, with the door on his back.

Father McElhone wasn't the only one who made mistakes. I made plenty. On one of the streets I had an easy assignment. The mother of a family phoned me, the day before, and said that she had a son who had fallen away from the Church, and would I please try to do something about it. She had talked, begged, and pleaded, but nothing happened. In a matter of this kind, a little tact goes a long way. You do not demand that the youth return to the grace of his God. You suggest. You listen. You sympathize. But most of all, you make him see that it is more profitable for him, for his soul, his peace of mind, his general health, if he returns to the Church of his forebears. In sum, the rewards are his.

Well, I visited the house, and when I arrived the mother and daughter and son were sitting in the basement. The son was holding a newspaper in front of him. I chatted with the mother and daughter, and then I got down to cases. When

I inquired if everyone attended Mass and the sacraments regularly, the mother answered yes and so did the daughter. The son sat behind his paper.

I reached over and slammed it down from between his hands.

"I'm talking to *you!*" I yelled.

He kept his two hands up as though they still held the newspaper. If looks could kill, I'd have been a dead man at that moment. He said nothing, just sat there with his lip curled in a sneer. I knew then that it was I who had made the mistake. I should have shown greater forebearance, despite the insulting provocation of the newspaper. He remained away from his religious duties for a long time after that, and his particular case never ceased to remind me of what a failure I had been.

In the census we always found—or rather, unearthed—a few marriages invalidly entered into. Reading that sentence over, I think I've backed into a statement. I mean to say "unmarried" in our eyes. When a priest learns about these things, he must straighten them out. I found one couple who had lived as common-law wife and husband for over twenty years. This was remarkable, but what was even more astounding was that they had ten children. They must have cherished each other dearly, or they would not have lasted together. And they must have loved all those children. But in over twenty years, they had not found twenty minutes to step into the church and have their union solemnized. If anyone can think of a more ridiculous situation than that, I'd like to hear it. Were they anti-God? No, they were not. Were they afraid of censure after so many years? They were not. What, then, was the reason? Carelessness, just plain chronic carelessness. They meant to get married, but it seemed that they never found time for it.

Another woman of fifty-six, who should have had her head examined, was found to be living in intimacy with an adopted son of eighteen. That damage had to be repaired, and believe me it was repaired quickly and permanently. I learned that the boy was the son of a woman who used to do the washing for the fifty-six-year-old woman. When the boy's mother died, the other woman adopted him. He was a big, strong fellow, and stupid. His adopted mother matched him mentally. I learned after questioning that neither wanted to be separated, so I married them. This made it possible for both to return to the sacraments.

After only two days of work in one census, I found ten children who had not yet been baptized. I confronted their mothers, and they told me that they would have baptized the youngsters long ago, but they were ashamed to have it done without being able to make an offering. I soon fixed that up. I brought the ten children to church, baptized them, and brought them home, and I never saw such delighted mammas in my life.

Social life in the rectory is, and has always been, limited. In my six years with Monsignor Sheppard it can be said to have been *very* limited. No parsonage is a home, ever. It's more like a small, exclusive hotel with few guest privileges. During my life as a priest I think I've missed the home atmosphere most of all. No one in a rectory knows anyone else inside out. No one knows your strengths, your weaknesses; no one stands between you and your daily sorrows.

You never have the companionship of children of your own. In fact, you learn quickly that you belong to everyone who needs you, and, in the same breath, you belong to no one. You have your own quarters. So do the others. You are, in a practical sense, one family under one pastor. Nevertheless, you are a stranger in that family—an individual, separate and independent in your actions and affections.

Sometimes, an aura of real home atmosphere seeps into a rectory. It may come on Christmas or in July. It may last an hour or a week; but when it comes you feel the warmth and cheerfulness of it, and you stand before it happily, permitting its rays to thaw your bones. Now and then, in the Monsignor's tenure, a distinguished personality would be entertained at dinner, and by the time the cook had brought in the soup the granite personality of the Monsignor had melted, and we curates felt that we were sitting in box seats at a brilliant performance. The dinner was always superb, always a fine example of what Nellie McCann could do with a skillet and a fire.

The conversation sparkled, and your eyes darted back and forth across the table like those of a spectator at a tennis match. The interchange of ideas and information, and the wit, made us dread to see the dessert arrive. Of course the core of everything was Old Ironsides himself. He channeled the conversation with the dexterity of a destroyer skipper who has just discovered that he's in a nest of U-boats.

The very chair he sat in, at those dinners, was famous in its own right because many years before, when Monsignor DeConcilio was pastor, he had sat there. DeConcilio was the author of the world-renowned Baltimore catechism, the first warming crumbs of Catholicity partaken of by most of us. Monsignor DeConcilio, at dinner one night, remarked to Father Mark Moslein, C.P., that, at the request of the hierarchy, he had just finished a catechism and sent it off.

"Undoubtedly," he said, buttering a square of bread, "it will go into the wastebasket and that will be the last I'll ever hear of it."

He was wrong. The first draft was published as he had

written it, and was used everywhere in the United States for the next fifty years without a single revision. Many attempts have been made to equal, or surpass, that little booklet but, so far, with little success. Each year a million new moppets, with great love of God and little understanding, begin to study that booklet anew.

Speaking about Nellie McCann's dinners brings me to the subject of Nellie herself. She completed the austerity which was so much a part of life in the rectory. She was a big woman, and very capable. She had a sizzling temper, and woe betide the girl in the kitchen who, by mistake, dumped the carrots into the vinegar. Her assistants were always coming and going, and the employment agency, kept busy with repeated phone calls for more girls, must have thought that a world war was going on in the kitchen.

We called Nellie "the Abbess." She was certainly an amazon, but she was exactly what the Monsignor wanted, and the matter rested right there. She was efficient—and how she was efficient! She knew where to buy and how much to buy and what the prices ought to be. All the chinaware, linen, and table silver that she bought in the long ago are still in the rectory and in excellent condition. In fact, I've often suspected that the actual layout of the rectory—one of the finest in the archdiocese—is partly a product of her practical mind. Unfortunately, she had more of the attributes of the irritated stepfather than the loving mother, and she seldom won a place in the hearts of any of the priests.

Between me and the other curates there was a spirit of friendship and fraternal charity. This helped to offset the feeling of tension which was always present in the rectory. Father Ratigan was an especial boon to me because he was always full of laughter and antics. When "Old Jasper" left, and wasn't coming back for a while, I have seen Father Ratigan jump up on the flat oak desks we had in our rooms and do a crazy dance with the most ridiculous gestures.

Sometimes when Father Ratigan put on a minstrel, his jokes were funny, but not prudent. One of our parishioners was a man named McInerney. He was a big man and a heavy drinker. One of the gags staged in one minstrel was, "Why is McInerney's nose like a gas meter?" and the answer was, "Because it registers more than it consumes." The joke was a home run, and the people rolled with laughter. But McInerney didn't like it, and he came around to complain to the Monsignor.

Father Barrett, for all his gruffness, had the soul of a poet, and it may be that he hoped to hide it. But all of us knew that he was very fond of poetry, and particularly the works of Father Tabb. In trouble and sickness, I never saw a fuller heart than Father Barrett's, and nothing could stop him from helping. At the same time he could wield a tomahawk and peel a scalp, which only goes to show that we're all wonderfully and fearfully made.

Each year St. Michael's produced two important plays, and Father Barrett used to coach these himself. During those days the parish established a record for the quality of these productions, and people came from all over to see them, not as an act of charity, but because the plays were that good. Well, every time a play was to begin rehearsals, Father Barrett would start to gripe and growl. He didn't want it; it was too much for him; let somebody else do it for a change; etc. But he always coached the plays, and, deep down, he loved every minute of it because the romantic and the dramatic were inside his soul.

The assignment that Father Ratigan and I drew was to go out and secure a good play without paying any royalty. In addition, we worked on the program alone, and had to dispose of tickets either through the mail or by peddling them from door to door. Of course the Old Man used to pit us against each other, praising the one who was selling more tickets, and needling the other to go out and beat him.

But the best man at this work was always Father Ratigan. When it came to getting a good script free, and then talking someone into giving him the sets and properties too, no one could excel him. When something was known to be impossible to get, Father Ratigan would go out and get it. In one play we needed a large number of small flags. They had to be different flags. There was no way that the play could be altered to get around this necessity. Father Ratigan had the nerve to go to New York, meet the original producer of the play, and talk him out of flags and sets and whatever teeth in his head may have been loose. When he sold tickets and advertisements, his feet fairly flew through the parish, and in the evening he'd come into the rectory with a list of patrons and advertisers that would make you gasp. Once the manager of the Majestic Theater in Jersey City said to me, "That man missed his vocation. He belongs in show business."

I played a joke on John once. I knew that, for all his flamboyant good humor, he was as naïve as an infant in a pit of rattlesnakes. At the time the big news was the Ku Klux Klan, which was broadcasting its special brand of venom all over the country. So, as I had some business with a local printer, I asked him if he'd strike off a letterhead with a skull and crossbones and, in large type, "Domain of the Imperial Wizard." He did, and on that letterhead I typed a threatening note to Father John Ratigan, and mailed it. Then I tipped off everyone in the rectory that it was coming.

Well, Ratigan read it, and you should have seen the commotion. He was all over the rectory, telling one and all that the Ku Kluxers were coming to get him. He had always had fleet feet, but he covered ground now as though the Imperial Wizard was hanging onto his cassock. He even called the Second Precinct Police Station and alerted the captain and all his command. When I thought that the joke had gone far enough, I called John aside and told him that it was all a joke. He surprised me. Instead of getting angry, he laughed heartily.

When it came my turn to put on a play, John was the man I had to follow. I followed his ways and means as closely as I could, but there was only one Father Ratigan. Once I put on *Smilin' Through*. I had all of two hundred dollars' worth of artificial flowers on the stage, and God help me if the Monsignor couldn't see an extra two hundred dollars coming in at the box office. But John helped, and I, as the baby of the family, made good.

One of the greatest helpers I had was Mrs. Charles Clancy, Lord rest her soul, who solicited many an advertisement and burned up all kinds of shoe leather to help the play succeed. When I went to New York to pick up donated scenery, I rode the truck with the truck driver. But we had a good dramatic society, and we made some fine amateur actors. Our Central Casting Bureau was at the back of the church, where I'd stand watching the parishioners leave Mass. If I saw a young man, or a young lady, who "looked" the type, I'd approach and invite that one to try out for the part. Sometimes it worked out. Sometimes it didn't. When it worked out, the people of the parish came in droves because they enjoyed seeing their neighbors on the stage. The names of our stars will mean nothing to you, but from my standpoint they roll more off the heart than the tongue. They were Catherine Treacy, Teresa Curtin, Mary Smith, William Clancy, Nora Wallace McNally, Irene Rochford Boles,

Walter Verbout, John Hassett, George Donahue, Catherine Carberry (now a Sister of St. Joseph), Lillian Shenan, and— ah, I'm taking up your time with names which are meaningless to you. They were great. No Broadway smash hit, on opening night, was more tremulous, more excited, and, once the curtain went up, more serene than ours. These people were real troupers.

The backbone of any parish is easy to locate. Just look for the Rosary Society, the Holy Name Society, and the sodality. There you have it. Without those three the parish is almost spineless. The Rosary Society is composed of the married women. The Holy Name Society is composed mostly of married men. The sodality is composed of single women. Today the Catholic Youth Organization embraces parts of all three, but we didn't have a CYO in the days I have in mind.

Each of these three, in its way, is as important as the other two. The married women work harder and can raise more money with less merchandise to sell than any group. The sodality is usually smaller in number, but they try harder to emulate their older sisters and mothers, and tomorrow they will be the Rosary Society. The Holy Name Society does not sponsor a cake sale or a rummage racket, but they are the fathers who make it possible for the mothers and the daughters to keep up the good church work.

The big event of the year, in Catholic Hudson County, is the Holy Name Parade. It takes place on the second Sunday of October, and no other event equals it in size or in importance. Every parish vies with every other parish to have the largest turnout of men. The arrangements are protracted, and nothing except the weather is left to chance. The mayor will be there, and all the commissioners, and often the governor of the state of New Jersey. There are bandstands, reviewing stands, and great crowds of women and children along the line of march. Mustached vendors walk up and down the curbing, selling balloons and peanuts. In Lincoln Park a great temporary altar has been set up for benediction after the parade.

Every man, woman, and child is dressed in his finest, and the gleam of the shoes would blind you. Many of the men, on this one occasion, wear high silk hats and swallow-tailed coats and carry canes. Some of the marshals ride horseback. Before the parade arrives, squad cars, their sirens muted for this happy occasion, cruise in low gear up and down the line of march to make sure everything is in readiness. Traffic has been stopped in all directions, and in the old days at Montgomery Street you'd see a line of trolley cars standing tip to tip like loaves of bread in a bakery.

A few of the men would have a "ball" or two before their contingent started, the better to oil the aging hinges and bring mellowness to the spirit. The bands would strike up; every man carried a little blue pennant which said, in white, HNS; and away they went, swinging along as proud as you please, glancing to left and right and smiling and doffing their hats. The horses of the policemen danced to the music, and in the crisp air of early autumn forty or more thousand men in the line of march publicly proclaimed their Catholicity and held aloft the Holy Name of Jesus Christ.

For a number of years Father Barrett had charge of the Holy Name Society, and his arrangements for the big day were meticulous. Three of us heard the confessions of the men the night before the parade, and on Sunday morning it was a feast for happy eyes to see the hundreds and hundreds of men leave their pews one by one in the center aisle to begin the day by taking the Lord into their hearts. Afterward Father Barrett addressed the men informally, explaining

126

where they were to march, how many to the rank, which men had been picked as captains, and so forth. He had only one warning: don't drink. He realized that, sometimes, the men stood in the warm sun for an hour before St. Michael's was called to join its proper division in the parade, and he wanted no inebriation—even slight. Most of the men honored his warning, but a few would find their throats parched, and they would run into a corner saloon for a quick one. When Barrett saw that, his anger rose, and he waited outside the saloon. As each man came out, Father Barrett snatched the little blue-and-white pennant from him and broke it over his knee. Severe? Yes, but the priest had asked only one thing of them, and he figured that it was the few men who disobeyed who were being unreasonable.

He was a hard man, but a just man. I remember one time that we were running a combination block dance and bazaar in the street at West Hamilton Place. It was his show, and he had his booths set up with kewpie dolls and blankets and bags of flour and groceries and a thousand and one items. The naked bulbs, strung on wires, lighted the late-summer sky, and Mrs. Beggs's orchestra pounded the proper beat for the dancers as the little children scurried in and out and chased each other through the crowds. Father Ratigan and I had nothing to do—that is, no work—and so we wandered through the crowd, saying hello to Jenny and John, and asking after the health of Aunt Margaret and Uncle Eddy. Once in a while, I would stop to play one of the wheels, feeling that there was no better way to spend my pittance than to have it go back to the Church. By accident I won a small prize. At that moment Father Barrett came up, and he flayed me unmercifully, charging that, by winning a prize, I had literally prevented someone else from getting it.

7

THE END of my baby-of-the-family training came in the middle twenties. As a reward for his fine work, Father Barrett had been made pastor of Sacred Heart Parish in Newark. For a time Father John Clark returned to St. Michael's. Then, in 1925, as you know, the old Monsignor died. Thousands saw him lying in state, and it was said that many came just to be sure that he was dead.

The new boss was Father Michael P. Corcoran. He had been pastor of St. John's in Newark, and there is no doubt that crowded St. Michael's came as a promotion. We all wondered what he was going to be like, and we soon found out. Father Mike was a giant of a man, about 250 pounds of geniality. He loved people, and people loved him. He was a bighearted Irishman, the son of a quarryman of Jersey City. On a bitterly cold day, like as not, you'd find him standing out in front of the rectory, his knuckles on his hips, in shirt sleeves. He was a born buff, and whenever the fire engines roared past Ninth Street, he ran as fast as he could to the front windows and watched them go by. In church, he was happiest doing traffic duty, that is, standing in back and making the parishioners walk down and take front pews when they wanted to sit in back pews.

When Father Mike arrived, one of the welcomers was Father Jack O'Malley, of neighboring St. Lucy's Church. He shook hands with Father Corcoran and said, "Mike, you fell into a tub of butter."

He was right. St. Michael's was a fine, rich parish. But the Holland Tunnel, linking New Jersey to New York, had not yet been blasted through, and Twelfth Street, one of St. Michael's most populous thoroughfares, had not been razed to make one of the tunnel approaches. Also, the big depression had not yet arrived to impoverish our people and do irreparable damage to our buildings. Father Mike was to see only the beginnings of these things.

In essence, I guess, Corcoran was the opposite of his predecessor. His regime was more open, less strict, than what we had been accustomed to. His special pets were the Holy Name Society and Federation, and he was intensely interested in their meetings. He introduced the envelope system for Sunday collections, and he installed modern machines for the counting of money. He also bought an Addressograph machine for making stencils of the names and addresses of all who lived in the parish, and this expedited the mail between the priests and the parishioners. He made improvements in the rectory, and he started major renovations of the church.

Perhaps I'd better tell you about the church repairs in some detail, first because it was a major "face lifting," and second because it is rare for a new pastor to plunge a church into heavy debt. It takes nerve; but, more than nerve, it takes plenty of heart, and Father Corcoran had it.

An old and close friend of the new pastor was Justin Mc-
Aghon, of Roselle, New Jersey. Mr. McAghon was a member of the firm of Southern and Marshall, New York build-
ers and contractors. It was he who introduced Father to a
man named Wilfred Anthony, a metropolitan architect, renowned for his church work. Anthony was a convert from
Episcopalianism and had a wonderful sense of color and was
passionately fond of the simple and the beautiful.

For days Mr. Anthony sat out in the church, just looking.
What he saw, besides the traditional interior, I do not know.
But I do know that he was a champion of the liturgy, understood the laws of the Church, and was a pioneer in the liturgi-
cal movement which was to improve and to beautify so
many old and great churches. When his plans came through,
they were breath-taking. They called for the removal of our
three wooden altars and the erection of three marble altars.
They also required an extension of the sanctuary with marble flooring, marble wainscoting, and a marble altar rail. This,
in turn, meant the removal of the first three rows of pews
and additional steel supports in the basement of the church
to hold the increased weight. A large marble baldachin
(canopy), supported by four marble columns of different
colors, was to surmount the altar. Walnut choir stalls were
to stand on either side of the sanctuary, and five large heavenly murals were to be painted above the wainscoting in the
sanctuary, forming a semicircle. In the rear wall, behind
the altar, was to be a big stained-glass window of St. Michael.
A huge rood cross was to be suspended from the ceiling, in
front of and above the altar, flanked by the grieving figures
of Our Lady and St. John. The tabernacle itself was to be
of pure bronze and cylindrical in shape. It was one of the first
of its kind, and when it was completed it was placed on ex-

hibition. Today you see many of them, but St. Michael's had one of the first.

As if this wasn't enough, the whole ceiling was to be replaced with new ribs and a new finish, and a brand-new lighting system, replete with Italian chandeliers, was to make the church more cheerful. Two new organs were to be built, one in the choir and one in the chancel, both to be controllable from the same console. The rest of the church was to be completely redecorated with generous use of genuine gold leaf.

If you are saying that it might have been just as easy to tear the church down and start from the foundation stones, you are with but slight exaggeration right. It was an enormous job. The Bishop approved the plans, and Father Corcoran let out the contracts. For the next year (1925–1926) we carried on Mass and services with scaffolding filling the church and bits of plaster pocking the aisles. When it was finished, we knew that it was worth it. Many an evening I stood in the rear of the church, marveling at the beauty of the new St. Michael's.

There was some criticism, of course. It was never aesthetic, though. It was economic. People said that we had no right to spend so much money in a parish that had obviously passed its peak. The work used up all our funds and put us in debt for more than twenty years. On the other hand, the church was old and needed repairs, and if Father Corcoran had waited, the same work would, right now, have cost 150 per cent more than it did.

Big Mike Corcoran wasn't satisfied. The moment the new church was finished, he started a high school and appointed me its first principal. By the time it was completed, I was first assistant to the pastor and, I hope, his strong right arm. He was as good to his priests as he was to his flock, and that is good indeed. It took so little to satisfy Big Mike. He could eat like a Percheron, and his favorite food was Canadian bacon and mountains of kale. His favorite amusement was to stand in the doorway of Fire Truck 2, on Ninth Street, and talk to the firemen. You could hardly say that Father Corcoran was a hard man to please.

Still, they criticized him for building the high school. They said he had put a yoke of debt on the parish by remodeling the church, and where, the critics wanted to know, were the high-school students coming from in a parish that was dying on its feet? The clock has answered them. Time has seen the paying off of heavy debts, and time has seen the high school enroll 500 students in seventeen classrooms. Right now it has over 1500 alumni. Ten parishes send their elementary-school graduates to St. Michael's high school. The school has an enviable reputation for scholarship and discipline and, to my personal exultation, has also made its mark in athletics.

In my opinion the Catholic high school stands as an oasis in the moral sand waste of the world. The high-school years of life are the final formative years. Whatever you are when you get out of high school is what you will be for the rest of your life. It represents the final chance for teachers and parents to mold fine men and women. There are no more chances after that because by the time the college years arrive the boy and the girl "know all the answers" to life's problems without having experienced any of them. When they get out of high school, they are beyond telling; they no longer want advice; they listen to their parents with elaborate, restrained impatience. They look upon their elders as old-fashioned and overly cautious. They talk of love and marriage and sex as though these were newly discovered.

132

They are seldom sure what they want to do with their lives, but they would like a career consisting of lots of money and no work. They bruise easily, and any form of criticism is, in reality, persecution. They want to be pampered and petted and stay out late on Saturday and stay in bed all day Sunday —until dinnertime.

If that's your idea of how to turn out high-school students, it isn't mine. I don't want to turn out women; I want to turn out ladies: ladies of poise and grace and wisdom regarding their great role in life. Good housekeepers; intelligent mothers; wives who can keep abreast of their husband's work, and who can keep a step ahead of him when it comes to keeping him in line. Ladies who will never, under any circumstances, forget their God and their Church and their duty. As for boys, I don't want to turn out sissies, little Lord Fauntleroys who will run from a punch in the nose. But I don't want to turn out bullies either. I want men to come out of our high school: men who will leave their mark in the field of public affairs or the Church or business. I want big, strong fellows who are unafraid of life and its terrors; fellows who will dare to blaze new trails when everyone else around them laughs with contempt; men who when they take a girl take her as a wife, with the blessings of Holy Mother Church, not as weak-chinned whiners who stand on street corners and boast of the newest conquest. If this country is to survive, you are going to need more and more men like that, and ladies like that.

Certainly, because of its inherent weakness, the public high school is not so effectively geared to turn out such a type of student. Despite the general excellence of its teachers the system itself tends to a gradual break down of authority, discipline, and morals. Even the recitation of an anemic prayer becomes the subject of heated controversy.

Horace Mann started it. In 1850 he eliminated God from the public schools, and God has been out on the sidewalk ever since. Read the crime statistics in America from 1850 until now (allowing for the increase in population), and you will see what happened when America told God that He had no place in a hall of learning. Today a major crime occurs in the United States every twenty-two seconds. Why? The answer is inarguable. Our public high schools turn out youths whose minds have been educated, but whose consciences are dead. Even a clumsy rustic, if he has an educated conscience, is less prone to commit crime than an honor graduate who knows everything except what is right and what is wrong. No wonder so many non-Catholic parents prefer to send their children to Catholic schools. Reverence and respect are indispensable supports of a healthy republic.

Someone—I forget who—once said, "Restrictions which permit the child to be taught geography, but not about the God who made the earth; botany but not about the God who clothed the flower; physiology but not about the God who built man; astronomy but not about the God who guides the stars; history but not about Divine Providence in human affairs; human laws but not the divine commands for human conduct"—restrictions such as these certainly do not make sense. A great American admiral (not Catholic) recently said that the astronomers could tell you all about the laws governing the millions of stars in the sky but they never tell you who laid down the laws.

In 1928 I read about a new spirit in the high schools, a spirit of liberalism, free speech, free thought. Many schools announced that every instructor could teach his own subject in his own way; no subject was forbidden; all students were to be encouraged to develop their own ideas and convictions in any way they thought best, disagreeing with their teachers if they felt so disposed. Why, that's like walking up to a half-grown puppy, patting him on the head, and saying, "Now go ahead and housebreak yourself in any way you see fit, and if you disagree with me that you should be house broken, the place is yours."

Within six months after the new, "liberal" type of education had been inaugurated, these things happened. In New York, a sixteen-year-old boy committed suicide and left a note saying that it was his conviction that life was "pointless and futile." In Brooklyn, a student jumped to his death. A sophomore at a Western college shot himself to death, saying that he had experienced all that life had to offer and therefore was better off dead. Without proper guidance, these pupils came to their own conclusions.

The teacher's function is still to teach; the student's, to be taught. Surrender to laxity under the guise of "freedom" is a betrayal of the student. Those who teach must be equipped not only to give the facts of science and history; they should also be able to draw lessons from these facts: lessons which should be helpful to the student later in life. A writer for the Philadelphia *Ledger*, over a quarter of a century ago, said it better than I could: "The best way to inculcate character is for the teacher himself to set a pattern which it is desirable to emulate. A teacher like Gummere at Haverford, or Gildersleeve at Johns Hopkins, was more than the most eloquent page of any printed text. Such a preceptor does not need to preach morality; he lives it, and his pupils see the light and get the inspiration."

Dr. Carl Holliday, of the University of Montana, put it another way: "Surrounding Tom, Dick and Harry with fine pictures, noble buildings and orchestras breathing forth delightful harmonies does not make Tom, Dick and Harry any less selfish, any less a cheat, any less a liar, any less a murderer at heart, if any in actual deed. Abe Lincoln could hardly have known an oratorio from a Yankee Doodle; he probably could not have made much distinction between the Sistine Madonna and a Chromo; but he was nevertheless a highly civilized man, supremely civilized because his moral emotions were so highly developed that his every thought and action seemed to have constantly in view a relation with the highest Good."

I think too that a Baptist minister of Springfield, Illinois, a Dr. Frank B. Cussey, hit the nail on the head when he said: "Catholicism is right when she says that the education of the mind and the heart cannot be separated. We all agree that to educate the mind and not the heart is to make the rascal. I recognize a justness as well as a correctness in Catholicism's fundamental thought, that religion is an integral part of education."

Recently Mr. J. Edgar Hoover, director of the Federal Bureau of Investigation, said: "No gift of the Rockefeller or Carnegie Foundations, or any other Christian denomination, can equal the gift presented to the American people by the Catholic Church. It has nearly 11,000 schools with nearly 3,000,000 pupils who are taught by 95,000 patriotic teachers. Not a single atheistic teacher is among them; not a single non-Christian or non-American principle is taught."

This is not to say that, now and then, our Catholic high schools do not turn out duds who are a credit to no one. Among the graduates there can be potential wrongdoers. We who teach are aware of that. Our batting average is not 1000, nor is it ever likely to be. But we feel, with deep pride, that there would be a great many more moral failures if it weren't for the Catholic schools.

When Father Corcoran appointed me the first principal of St. Michael's High School, it was, to me, a challenge. I had had a little experience teaching at Seton Hall, but organizing and administering a high school, one that was just now coming into being, was a tough assignment and a grave responsibility.

When you're young, and you like your work, you have lots of zip and go. I tackled everything with tremendous zeal and determination. I had confidence that, within a short time, our high school would be known and respected in the state. I didn't know it at the time, but I was to stay in my post for the next thirteen years, and in that time I was to see many hundreds of young men and ladies come into our school pale and uncertain, and go out into the world bright and full of confidence.

Probably the most important factor in the success of the school was the fact that Father Corcoran permitted the word to get around that my decisions, whatever they might be, were his decisions. The moment that this was understood, it killed all appeals and strengthened the power of the office of principal.

At that I didn't expect smooth sailing, and I wasn't disappointed. What I planned for my darlings was one thing; what they planned was often quite another thing. I quickly realized that if we were to combine good studies with good discipline, somebody was going to have to get tough, and that somebody was me. We had hardly opened the school when the first complaint came in. A freshman from Ninth Street found some bullets on a winter day and thought it would be fun to drop them into his mother's kitchen range and run. He ran all right, and his mother wasn't far behind him because, in a minute, the house was full of flying dinner plates, and a crowd gathered in the street thinking that a gang was rehearsing a private war on the premises. The explosions stopped after a while, and Mother went back inside very cautiously. When her fright wore off, she vaguely remembered seeing her precious son standing across the street bursting with laughter. So his mother called him in and questioned him. The boy looked innocent and shocked that she would suspect him. (Don't they all!) She sent him over to my office, and with a little prodding he confessed.

"I just thought it would be fun," he said.

"Tell me," I said quietly, "are you playing hooky from an insane asylum?"

"No, Father."

"Suppose one of those bullets killed your mother?"

"I didn't think of that."

"How crazy do you have to be before they send the Black Maria for you?"

"I don't know, Father."

"I ought to dismiss you from the school, but I'm going to give you one more chance."

"Thank you, Father."

"Don't thank me. Thank your mother. She's the one who has to put up with you. But let me tell you this, Johnny: one more prank, and out you go."

"Yes, Father."

He left with that head-down, spurious contriteness which a teacher gets to know so well. At that moment all of them look as though they had vowed to spend the rest of their lives on their knees, making atonement. But they hardly get out of the office before they meet a pal and grin.

"You shoulda seen the way I handled McWilliams."

It wasn't long after that when an Erie Railroad detective called on me. Two of my bright-eyed prodigies, he said, had been caught up in the wheelhouse of a ferryboat that had

138

been tied up to its slip. They were just getting ready to ring down for full speed ahead when the law changed it to full speed astern. Of course one of the two was my old friend of the bullets. Since he was a second offender, I should have tossed him out of school, but I was afraid that, in effect, I would be giving him an assist to a life of crime. So, instead, I called him into my office, turned his back to me, raised my cassock, and gave him a hoist in the "slats" and hoped that he wouldn't be able to sit down for a month. I had a spare kick left, so I gave that one to the other boy.

It wasn't more than a month later when a man from the Public Service Co-ordinated Transport walked in with my two stalwarts. All I could do was sit and mumble, "What now?" My brain was full of flying bullets and ferryboats racing all over the Hudson River. The man said that the boys had walked into the Hoboken trolley terminal, boarded a vacant trolley, and driven it two blocks before the police caught up with them. I thanked the officer for turning the problem over to me instead of arresting them, as they deserved. When the cop left, I called the mother of my number-one boy in. The second boy had a guardian, and I called him in too.

Believe me, it was quite a session. I told the mother of the bullet boy that, as far as I was concerned, he was hopeless in both scholastic marks and deportment, and that I was dismissing him at once. Her shoulders sagged a little, and she said that she guessed there was nothing else that I could do— that she didn't blame me. Then I spoke to the guardian of my number-two boy, and I told him that one more misdemeanor would mean expulsion. I had no more trouble with that boy through the rest of the four-year course. He served with distinction in World War II and is now a serious, sedate, and well-informed man.

After a couple of years, I began to realize that we were wrong to take graduates from our own and other grammar schools without some added qualification. Too many youngsters were enrolling in our high school and "dying" in the first mid-term examinations. The mortality rate was much too high, and, accordingly, I set up a standard of admission that required the student to have a general average of 80 per cent in the last grade of grammar school. This eliminated some boys and girls from our own grammar school as well as those from other parishes, but it also eliminated a lot of failures in our freshman year. We still have some failures, but the number is not alarming.

Years of observing students has shown me several truths. As a nation, we are not so virile as we used to be. The student today is not so hardy as his father was. Unless watched closely, the student of today tends to spread his activities too thinly, over too many interests. Parents do not give the child the supervision he needs. No matter how hard the sisters work on their charges, that work can be canceled in the home.

Every Catholic high school has an inward and an outward life. It matches the inward and outward life of man. It is in the theater of our inmost soul that the great drama of life is played. It is not what we see, or hear, or read, that is important: it's the interpretation of these things in the heart of man that counts. The sole spectators of these events are God and our conscience.

As part of the inward life, we established a sodality for the young men and ladies of the school. We had the permission of the pastor and the approval of the bishop, and our sodality was affiliated, through the Jesuit provincial, with the mother sodality in Rome. This made available to us all the rich spiritual advantages which accrue to the parent organization. The aims of this sodality were personal holiness, the sanctification of our neighbors, and the defense of the Church. We knew that if we put God in the hearts of the young, the roots of life would be well nourished, and the tree would grow up sturdy and clean.

At the proper time the students were received into the sodality in a beautiful ceremony. As their queen, they chose Our Lady, knowing well that if they kept close to Her they would never be far away from Her Divine Son.

Part of the ceremony of induction, as recited, went like this:

"Our Lady is keenly interested in this occasion and in the consecration you are about to make. Looking down from her throne as Queen of Heaven, she sees you gathered about her altar, determined to consecrate your lives to her special service.

"She is smiling upon you, for, while others choose to serve the world, to follow fashion and vanity, to pledge their allegiance to wealth and power, you are to dedicate yourselves to her, the Mother of God and of men.

"She is especially pleased that you are to serve her in her Sodality. The Sodality, through the centuries of its existence, has given to the world men and women saints; it has given the church popes and kings, queens, and abbesses; it has counted among its members distinguished laymen and laywomen of every nation of the earth. It has never tired of singing the praises of Mary and of lifting thousands of souls to a closer imitation of her purity, her virtue, her service to Christ.

"Mary expects of you, her devoted children, a special service. Others may serve her tolerably well. You must serve her splendidly. You must spread the knowledge and love of her Son throughout the world. Those who love Mary serve her Son and spread His glory throughout the world—the great world of the missions, the intensive world of their own parish or school.

"You must serve and love the church, of which she is the Queen and Mother and which alone, in the face of a world that forgets Mary, honors and loves her.

"Singular privileges are yours as Sodalists of Our Lady. Rich indulgences are easily gained. You have the honor of association with millions of Sodalists all over the world. And you know that, by your consecration, you attain a nearness to Christ and Our Blessed Mother for which those not so privileged are justified in envying you.

"Yours is a great honor. Heaven is watching for the moment of your consecration. And Heaven expects you to be worthy of your dignity."

Afterward they elected their own officers, and the moderator appointed the various committees. Chief among them were Our Lady's Committee, the Eucharistic Committee, the Literary Committee, and the Social Life Committee. Every month we had a detailed agenda, and each member had an assignment to complete before the next meeting. We had forums and once a month a corporate Communion, followed by breakfast downstairs in the church auditorium. The sodality also sponsored the Knights and Handmaids of the Blessed Sacrament, and these members pledged themselves to receive Holy Communion once a week, and if they missed a week through some inadvertence they received Communion twice on the following week.

Almost from the start, I favored the general assembly in the morning. It served as a transition from street to school and put the students more in a mood for schoolwork. At 8:30 the entire student body met in the auditorium and began a recitation in English of the little office of the Blessed

Virgin. Then, using the music of a popular song, they sang lyrics written for Our Lady. After that, the names of all the students were placed in a box, and three were selected at random to go up on the stage and perform. They could carry on in any way they chose—by singing a song, reciting, or making an impromptu speech. The purpose of this, of course, was to develop self-confidence and poise.

I had always felt that our boys and girls were too apathetic; they showed neither alertness nor aggressiveness. It reminds me of the story they tell about the divinity student who loved to sleep. The excitator came in one morning and shook the student and said, "Now, Michael, your guardian angel is on one side of you, telling you to get up, and the devil is on the other side of you, telling you to stay in bed. Now, which one are you going to follow?"

Mike thought it over for a moment, yawned, turned over and said, "Ahhh, let them fight it out between themselves."

Leadership cannot be developed in that way. It is by reading, writing, thinking, and talking that we forge ahead in life, and there is no substitute for those things. I had an old English professor who used to say, "Read and meditate; read and meditate; then read and write."

For thirteen years I plugged this theme before student bodies. Whether it did any good I cannot say, but I felt confronted with apathy every day of every school year. Maybe I was flailing the wind, but I don't like to think so. You can plant a seed, and you can nourish it, but only God can make it grow.

The general assembly also gave me the forum that I sought, to comment at length on some thought expressed by a student, to give a message to the whole school, and sometimes to dress them down for infractions of the rules. One afternoon a policeman reported to me that some of the high-school boys were shooting craps on the corner during lunch hour. When he had upbraided them for it, they heaped denunciation on him and ran. The next morning I had the cop in for general assembly. I told the whole school what the charge was and asked the officer to go down into the student body and pick out the culprits for me. He did, and in the presence of the student body and all the sisters I took the guilty apart verbally and suspended them from school. There were no more corner crap games for a long, long time.

On another morning I came into general assembly with jets of steam hissing from every pore. They had seen me angry, but never this angry. I took off my coat and hurled it across the stage. I believe that there was very little breathing done in the next ten minutes, because I tore into them and I never paused in my tirade. The day before, someone had started a fire in a paper basket in one of the boy's rest rooms. The fire itself wasn't dangerous, but the smoke seeped out into the corridors and into the study rooms and nearly caused a panic.

When I finished roaring, I was out of breath. The anti-climax came, however, when one of the boys went up on the stage and picked up my coat, and the contents on the floor. I glared at him as icily as I could, but—whether it was mock courtesy or brassy presumption I do not know—he stared at me steadily and dusted the coat and put the items back in the pocket and then, with a little bow, handed them to me.

The outward life of the school was taken up with study, occasional dances, and athletics. We started with basketball, and from the very beginning the team was coached by Johnny Griffin. Johnny was an alumnus of St. Michael's grammar school, and after he graduated from Seton Hall College I engaged him to coach the basketball team. He produced many championship teams, and today he is our director of athletics. We were lucky, too, to acquire the services of Tom Finn, an idealist to his heels and the greatest track enthusiast of our times. He started with us around 1936, and from that day onward St. Michael's became well known in the spiked-shoe department. In recent years we have gone in for baseball, and, although St. Michael's has yet to produce a pennant winner, our boys have given a good account of themselves. We also have intramural sports, and through them much school spirit has been developed.

I feel pardonably proud of what I've done with the high school, but let me tell you that I am of small importance in that field when I compare my work with that of the sisters. This is not a becoming modesty. The Sisters of Charity of Convent Station, New Jersey, were and are the heart and core of the high school. A priest can do some good; he can oversee and direct, but he can be in only one place at one time. The sisters are everywhere, all the time. The only life the sisters had was the students. They had dedicated themselves to teaching, and they spent their lives and their hearts teaching. Many and many a girl got her first inspiration to enter religious life while sitting at the feet of a patient nun, and many a boy got to thinking about the priesthood because of the holy character of the sister who taught him.

It is impossible to describe how much the sisters have done. You would have to come to St. Michael's, and be with one of them from the time of the first morning devotions, through the school day and its multitudinous problems, through the long evening when they correct the school papers and plan the curriculum for tomorrow, to the point of exhaustion when they make their nightly devotions in their own chapel, to understand. And even then, you would have seen them on but one day, and you would have to multiply

145

their work many hundreds of times to gain a glimmer of understanding. After that you would come to me and say, "I saw it, but it's impossible. No human being can do that much work in one day."

I think that Sister Mary Faith Schuster, of the Order of St. Benedict, described the teaching sister very well.

"Seek God in the midst of men," she said. "Enter into solitude of heart facing forty children every hour. Taste singleness of heart in the midst of seeming compromise. Give your pupils the wine of God's strong life, the deep tender current of the love of the Mystical Body, and dare to meet the educational requirements of your state. . . .

"God is present in His living creatures just as truly as in the quiet of green leaves blowing in a convent garden . . . and if talking of the One we love nourishes the love, then there is no better place for growth in the love of God than a twentieth-century Catholic classroom. Children love Him too, and if we draw out the thoughts they think we shall find them beautiful, and we shall create the strongest possible bond between teacher and students. . . . God is in the classroom, in the hearts of the slow to understand, in the shining eyes of those who are a little quicker.

"With zest and joy we Marys with the pointer and the red pencil must know Him in the sacrament of the moment's search for the right algebra answer, the true source of any one of the wars of history, the analysis of a poem. We must find and drink deeply of the water of Siloe too, even while for Christ's sake we are trying to be all things to the plaid-shirted little branches of the Vine of Christ. . . .

"Christ was among the children, the poor, the crowds, and the rich young men just as truly as He was alone on the mountainside during His lifetime. I know that He is in my classroom, and I adore him in the soul of each child as we

146

seek Him together in the day's program. And I think that we teachers can say to our Sisters in the Cloister: 'We too have found Him whom our soul loveth, and His mercy endureth forever. . . .' And some day—oh, some day—it would be lovely to see an American-born teaching Sister, not a foundress or a pioneer, with chalk on her veil and ink on her fingers standing on a pedestal in a parish church with her sisters Scholastica, Margaret Mary, Therese. She would prove to us that the pointer and the grading pencil can express the overflowing of love for God."

Sister's hope is a noble one, that someday an American teaching sister may be canonized by the Church and, with "chalk on her veil and ink on her fingers," stand as a pedestaled statue with the other saints. If we pray hard enough, some of us may live to see it. It seemed regrettable that the number of sisterly vocations has not kept pace with the growth of our schools. Most Catholic high schools, because of this shortage of sisters, do not have completely clerical faculties. St. Michael's now employs many lay teachers, and has done so for many years. I am proud to say that these teachers are doing fine work, and perfect harmony prevails between them and the sisters.

The priests of the parish have also been members of the faculty of the school and, from its very inception, have gladly taught the religious courses in its various branches. I taught religion in the senior grade until a few years ago when the pressure of many other duties made it impossible for me to be in class regularly. So I gave it up. In any case, let me observe that neither Father Al Merity nor myself could ever compete with Father Joe Murphy because Father Joe always gave marks to his students ranging between 90 and 100. Every teacher knows the difficulty of setting down ability in the form of numbers, but to have so many students always at the top is one of the scholastic mysteries of the age. I would not, for a moment, permit myself to think that Father Murphy is just a "good Joe" when it comes to giving out marks. That cannot be. It must be because, with some mysterious magnetism, he attracts only the finest of religious students. It must be.

However, back in the late twenties, when the high school was first opened, the curates who worked with me were Father Harold Fitzpatrick and Father Edward McGuirk. Father Fitzpatrick is now the pastor of St. Bridget's Church in Jersey City, and Father McGuirk is pastor of St. John's Church in Bergenfield, New Jersey, where he did excellent work in erecting a new church. Father Fitzpatrick was the kind of priest who has a cosmopolitan interest in everything about life; the kind of priest another priest would like to "winter and summer with." Father McGuirk was called "Bullets" because of his great size and unusual muscular development. He was probably the best clerical golfer in the diocese.

Later he was transferred to Holy Trinity Church, in Hackensack, where the well-known Monsignor Brown was pastor. The Monsignor had a sense of humor that ran toward practical jokes, and he played these jokes on his curates. Excuse me, not only on his curates but on any other priest he might meet. Sometimes the staid priests from other parishes were uncomfortable in the Monsignor's presence, because they didn't know at what moment a cigar might explode in their faces or the chair might collapse.

He must have been one up on Bullets McGuirk, because Father McGuirk was waiting to get even one morning when he accompanied the Monsignor to the funeral of a priest. When they went to a room in the rectory to vest, McGuirk noticed a bottle of whisky on a side table. Now there is nothing wrong about that, because some people appreciate that type of refreshment, but Father McGuirk noticed that the Monsignor had spotted the bottle, and he knew that some sort of joke would be played.

So while they were out front chatting with other priests, Father McGuirk sneaked back into the room to take a look. Sure enough, the whisky was gone. McGuirk wasted no time. He knew where to look, right in the Monsignor's *porté-de-main* bag. And when he looked, there it was, nestling comfortably between vestments. He removed the bottle, and scoured around until he found another exactly like it. This one was empty. Down in the kitchen, he found some Flit, and he poured the insecticide into the empty bottle and placed it in the "boss's" bag.

When the funeral was over, Father McGuirk drove the Monsignor home and even carried his bag to his room. The Monsignor never said a word about the whisky. Neither did McGuirk. The priest went back to his own room and cocked an ear against the door, waiting for results. He didn't have to wait long. Pretty soon the priest heard the tentative cough that signaled the desire to have one before dinner, and then call up the host and tell him what fine "spirits" he kept on hand.

In his room Father McGuirk was roaring with laughter until the tears came. He had foxed the old fox himself, and now they were even. When they sat to dinner, the Monsignor's face was an outraged scarlet. He glared at Father McGuirk for a moment, and then he accused him openly of tampering with the whisky. Father McGuirk didn't deny it. He said nothing; he just put on a look of injured innocence. The old pastor knew then that he would have to get up awfully early in the morning to get the better of McGuirk, so there were no more practical jokes involving McGuirk.

It is difficult to believe, even now, but after a few years in St. Michael's Father Corcoran was getting close to death. This giant of a man, with his great hamlike hands, was near the end of the road. He became ill of heart disease and went across the street to St. Francis Hospital. He was under the strictest orders not to get out of bed. However, when Holy Name Sunday came along, St. Michael's contingent passed the hospital, and Father Corcoran couldn't resist the opportunity to take a quick look at his boys. No one was in the room. He got out of bed, stood at the window a moment with longing in his eyes, and then he got back in bed. However, when the nurse returned, she knew that he had been out of bed, and when he looked dumfounded at her knowledge she told him why. The imprint of the wire screen was on his nose. Later he was transferred to St. Michael's Hospital in Newark, where, after lingering awhile, he died.

Ah, but he was a wonder of a priest. He was big in heart and big in limb, and he appreciated anything that was done for him. And how he loved to eat and talk! He wasn't much of a sleeper, and he'd keep you up until the wee hours, discussing this and that, if you didn't break away. Every night after nine o'clock, he led a raid on the kitchen icebox, and we'd sit at the kitchen table with him, eating and talking. One of his friends was John Matthews, the noted lawyer and orator; and when Matthews visited the "Club 252" (the rectory address on Ninth Street) no one wanted to go to bed. It was during those years that I put on extra weight, weight which had to come off the hard way.

Any assignment that Father Corcoran gave you, he gave you carte blanche with it. You could execute it any way you chose. And if he was pleased with your work, he wanted you to know it, and he wanted everyone else to know it too. He was with us only three years, but St. Michael's is the richer for his having passed our way, and the people of St. Michael's will not soon forget him. I am sure that his many good works preceded him to heaven and pleaded eloquently for him as he stood expectantly before God, his eternal Father.

My classmates pointed out that I had buried two pastors and it was about time I got the hatchet myself. Frequently, when a new pastor comes in, the curates are transferred. But I was lucky. Just as old Monsignor Sheppard had kept me in his service, and Father Corcoran kept me in his, so did the new pastor, Monsignor William A. Griffin, retain me. He was the diocesan director for the Propagation of the Faith, and he had preached from every pulpit in the diocese. He had conceived a great love for St. Michael's, and when Mike Corcoran died, he applied for the rectorship. In most parishes, the bishop makes the appointment; but throughout the United States a certain number of the larger parishes have "irremovable" or "permanent" rectorships. A vacancy in any of these is filled by a concursus, or competitive examination. St. Michael's was such a parish, and Monsignor Griffin's heart was so set on the rectorship that he took the examination and won the appointment.

Ten years later, when he was appointed Auxiliary Bishop of Newark, I know that he would have preferred to stay on in St. Michael's. As he traveled around the diocese, he would always refer to the manner in which things were done at St. Michael's. And later, when he became Bishop of Trenton, I met priests who told me about his fond references to St. Michael's.

His advent marked the coming of a new type of pastor. Long years of meditation had kept his entire life anchored to priestly ideals. And, as he was, so he took others to be. He had kept himself on a sort of pedestal, and he assumed that everybody else was up there with him. He treated his assistants as junior partners in a large going concern, of which he was the senior partner. All shared a joint responsibility for the general welfare of the whole concern—the betterment of the people and the salvation of souls.

He had learned to rule himself, and now he could rule others. In a way, it wasn't easy to "rule" the others because his curates were endowed with a healthy sense of independence; they were men whom he did not appoint, and who were not bound to him by any vow of obedience.

Unfortunately, he was not a well man. He suffered from a bad gall bladder and nervous exhaustion. At his request, the Bishop appointed me as administrator during the Monsignor's illness. He had two operations, one of which was performed by Dr. Raymond Sullivan in St. Vincent's Hospital, New York. After the first few years, he convalesced and enjoyed good health throughout the rest of his pastorate.

He had spirituality, dignity, and geniality in equal parts, and he was in great demand as a speaker. One of his enduring works was the foundation of the Lay Apostolate, an organization of young women interested in leading a spiritual life. With great fidelity the Monsignor met with them every Monday evening, and he discoursed with them on the principles of the spiritual life. From these young ladies he recruited more vocations for the religious sisterhoods than any other priest in the diocese. In this work he had a fine assistant, Mary Walsh of Harrison, New Jersey, and with her cooperation girls from St. Michael's and other parts of the diocese joined the group and attended the conferences.

Monsignor Griffin had a special interest in the sick and the poor. He was never too busy to see them or, for that matter, to hand out money. The Sunday school became his pride and joy. He was the first pastor to set up a kindergarten in

St. Michael's grammar school. He laid a new floor in the high school and installed a cafeteria in the auditorium. He carried out renovations in the convent at a cost of $10,000.

Two major things occurred during his pastorate which hurt the parish considerably. One was the opening of the Holland Tunnel and its ramps, which wiped out several hundred families on Twelfth Street—the very heart of the parish. Second, this exit hurried others on to move out of St. Michael's. The other event was the Great Depression. Property owners found themselves unable to pay their taxes, and they forfeited their homes to the city. From that time on a gradual deterioration set in, seriously undermining realty values in the parish. Families evicted from homes in other parts of Jersey City were moved into the empty ones in St. Michael's Parish, and these new families did nothing to keep the houses looking nice, and the city, which now owned them, did less. After a period of years, the flats seemed to disintegrate through neglect. They began to look like dirty shadows. And this, too, gave impetus to the flight from St. Michael's to newer, brighter sections of the city. The old Horeshoe, as we knew it, was dying. It will be a protracted death scene, and it will continue to gasp for another twenty or thirty years, but the doom is on its face. The grandeur is gone, and today I can stroll down Grove Street, or Erie, and count the flats with the blind, gaping eyes. As it dies, a bit of me dies with it, because this was an old-fashioned Irish section about which one could write movies and books. Anything that could possibly happen—and some things which couldn't— have taken place in the Horseshoe.

An event of great magnitude to us was the consecration of Thomas J. Walsh as Bishop of Newark. It was important because he, a lean, spectacled man with bright eyes and a slow, almost thoughtful smile, was known as an educator and a builder. Too often, you see, we have churchmen who dwell in such a deep world of the spirit that the bricks and straw of life are neglected. Bishop Walsh was not of these. His spirit was great and deep, but he wanted to build minds, and he wanted to place brick upon brick, for the love of God.

He was not a hearty man. Few indeed belonged to the circle of his friends because that's the way he wanted it. Not long after he became bishop, Newark was created as an archdiocese and he was made archbishop. And all of us, as priests, soon felt the impact of Archbishop Walsh. He had three loves: education, building, and music. I am only guessing when I say this, but I believe that he built more schools, more convents, more homes for children and for the poor, than all his predecessors.

He dared to do.

He built an imposing chancery office in Newark at the beginning of his episcopate, and, because the office was centrally located, it suddenly became easy to transact the general business of the diocese. It gave you a feeling that the strings of all the parishes led to one place, and were held in one hand. And that, in turn, gives a priest confidence. He pledges obedience to those in authority, and it is a warming feeling to know where the authority lies.

Archbishop Walsh's recurring thought was that the greatest Christian work all of us can do is "the service of the poor." And in 1930, in the midst of the Depression, he organized the Mount Carmel Guild. This guild has twenty-eight departments which are permanently alerted to the needs of the poor, the sick, those in need of shelter, and those who require social or religious rehabilitation.

For a while, the work of the guild was supported by one-dollar subscriptions, but soon the cries of the poor and the hungry mounted as the depression deepened, and His Excellency found it necessary to go to the general public and beg for money. He amended the constitution of the guild and appointed young, vigorous priests as vice-moderators in each district. He depended upon them to direct the campaign and raise the funds.

Somehow it didn't seem to occur to anyone that the Mount Carmel Guild was a highly unusual organization, because, in effect, it was doing the community's work. The poor, the ill, the destitute, are the problems of mayors and commissioners. But Archbishop Walsh wanted to do the work himself, and he did. His express order was that race, creed, or color was to mean nothing in the work of the guild; that we were to help anybody who needed help.

I was appointed vice-moderator in Jersey City, and after canvassing for money over a period of three days I stopped, and inaugurated my own plan. My own collections for the guild were pitifully small, and I had a feeling that the only way to make them big would be, first, to solicit help instead of funds. So I organized a group called the Bishop's Committee, and I sent invitations to the most powerful men in Jersey City to meet with me in St. Michael's auditorium on January 24, 1932. They accepted, and what a clan I had before me on that day! I had the finest lawyers, doctors, judges, businessmen, merchants, politicians, you ever saw.

As chairman, we elected Thomas J. Brogan, then corporation counsel of the city, and later chief justice of the New Jersey supreme court. As vice-chairmen, we had Judge Charles M. Egan of the court of common pleas; Alexander Sullivan, president of the Jersey City Board of Education; Dr. James Nugent, superintendent of the Jersey City schools, and Dr.

James Norton, chief medical examiner. As recording secretary, we had Richard McGrath; as financial secretary, Civil Service Commissioner Maurice J. Cronin.

The whole campaign began to look a lot better. Under these generalissimos we appointed a corps of twenty captains who knew the various sections of the city inside and out. They were empowered to select their own aides, as the work demanded. John J. Beggans, director of public safety, took care of the city police and firemen; Chief Patrick Dolan took care of his Hudson County police; Chief William Clossey was responsible for his Boulevard police; Dr. James Nugent and Mr. Sullivan would canvass the schoolteachers; Egan and others would be responsible for the lawyers; Dr. Norton, the doctors and dentists. The aides of the captains would conduct a house-to-house appeal. On top of these, we made up a special list of substantial donors, and the chairman and vice-chairmen were responsible for contacting them.

Well, with that kind of assistance, how can you miss? Many of the districts, with the exception of Newark, had little money to turn over that first year. But we had $24,600. And in the years that followed, I conducted ten campaigns for the guild, and we raised a total of $300,000.

In 1943, at the request of the President of the United States, all drives were merged into one. The Associated Catholic Charities, in Jersey City, merged its goals with that of the Community Chest, and since then as vice-chairman of the Chest, I have been identified with it and its work. In the first nine years the Associated Catholic Charities has received substantial sums of money from the Chest.

In 1936 the Archbishop asked for $1,000,000 with which to build a new seminary at Darlington, New Jersey. Directors were appointed for each county, and Hudson fell to me. We arranged a series of dinners, and when we had one in

Hoboken 1200 persons were present. The drive closed with a net of around $1,500,000.

The Archbishop was seventy-five years of age when he decided that he would finish Sacred Heart Cathedral in Newark. This cathedral had been building for fifty years, and it needed at least $5,000,000 more for completion and another $1,000,000 for furnishings. His last great goal was to finish the cathedral in 1953, when the diocese would be one hundred years old. He wanted to dedicate it then, as his final great work. But the builder was called before the work was finished. In June, 1952, Archbishop Thomas J. Walsh died in the early hours of the morning. Now, more than ever, his flock of over 1,000,000 people is determined that the cathedral shall be finished—and on time for the centennial.

During the thirties I was kept about as busy as possible. I was in the school every morning at 8:30 and stayed until three or four in the afternoon. I was handling fund drives, making sick calls, arranging marriages, saying Masses, hearing confessions, "umpiring" domestic troubles, and, in general, keeping on the move. This is not to say that my fellow curates were idle. They worked just as hard, but I had by this time my finger in so many pies that I could not drop any of them.

On the Feast of St. Blase, one year, I was out in the church in the evening, blessing the throats of the parishioners who lined the altar rail with their babies and children. When the services were over, I went to my room to rest. My feet were up when the bell rang. It was raining out, and past nine o'clock, and I couldn't imagine who would be calling.

I went downstairs and opened the door, and there were Pat Kane and two of his bodyguards. Pat was a neighborhood character, and, as far as size goes, he could have played fullback on Notre Dame. I invited him in, along with his boys, and sat them in the parlor. I asked Patty what was on his mind.

"Father," he said in a whisper that rattled the priestly paintings on the wall, "I clean forgot that this is St. Blase Day, and I wanted to know if you'd bless me t'roat."

I went out into the church and came back with the red stole and the blessed candles. Patty got down on his knees and then ordered his two torpedoes to do likewise. On his way out, he was a happy and grateful man.

"Father," he said seriously, "any time you want anything done, just let me know. If you want somebody bumped off, get in touch with me and I'll take care of it."

It was a lovely offer, a sort of fair-trade offer. I bless his throat, and in return he'll cut one for me.

A number of men in St. Michael's are on the police force, and one in particular is a big, husky man who would stare down a squad of bank robbers without blinking. Nothing could ever make him flinch. Did I say nothing? Well, one night he came into the rectory, and, whereas normally he was oozing bravado, now he was pale and nervous. In fact, when I asked him to sit down, I had to permit him a few minutes to catch hold of himself.

"Well," he said, "every time I start for here, Father, I lose my nerve. But this time, after walking around the block two or three times, I said to myself, 'You might as well go in.' So here I am."

"Well, what is it I can do for you?"

"Oh, well, Father, I've come to arrange for my marriage."

It was then my turn to laugh. If you could have seen the hulk of him, bowled over by a little woman! I soon had him at his ease, and then he began to enjoy the situation as much as I. After that, the rest seemed easy to him until the day of the ceremony, when he shook like a bowl of Jell-O in a tornado.

Another marriage I'll never forget was scheduled for four o'clock in the afternoon. Well, four came, and the bridegroom was there but not the bride. At 4:15 he began to pace the floor. At 4:30 the friends of the couple began to get restless in the pews. At 4:45 the organist was still trying, but was running out of music. At 5 o'clock the bride, somewhat flustered, arrived on the arm of her father.

I went through with the ceremony and, after it was over, the mystery was explained. The bride, a pretty Italian girl, was leaving her house with her father, and as she reached the sidewalk one of her former suitors stepped out of the crowd and slapped her face. The father of the girl hauled off and stiffened the ex-suitor. No one in the crowd knew what, exactly, had happened, but soon the whole neighborhood was pouring out of the tenements to get into the fight. It was a wild free-for-all, and someone put in a call to police headquarters. Soon a whole squad of cops was on the scene, trying to untangle bodies and trying to find out, in a bedlam of accents, who started it. The police were just about getting matters organized when someone turned in a fire alarm, and, in nothing flat, the engines were all over the block.

How the bridal party ever managed to live through all this, and show up at the altar *only* one hour late, is something I will never understand.

8

THE ROARING twenties gave way to the groaning thirties. Overnight, the rich became poor, and the poor became destitute. The resources of the St. Vincent de Paul Society and the Mount Carmel Guild were strained to the utmost. The rectory bell rang day and night, with formerly proud people standing outside begging for food and clothing. Many times it hurt the heart just to answer the bell. It is a terrible thing to see a big, healthy Irishman in a helpless condition; his hands empty, his wife weeping, his children staring up at him in silence, knowing that he never failed to feed them and certain, in their hearts, that he will not fail now. I saw more big hands work convulsively into fists and then straighten out impotently than I ever want to see again. What hurts more than the poverty is the helplessness of standing still. I saw men break down and sob from sheer helplessness. They didn't want to beg, they didn't want to steal—but it was one or the other.

No one was ever turned away from St. Michael's empty-handed; and that includes the chronic dead beats who have been coming to the door whining for thirty years. We had, and still have, our quota of those. In my mind, I have the thought that Christ comes to the door in the guise of the needy stranger, and the one that I turn away might be the one the Master sent to me. That's why I can't turn my back to a plea for help. If I did, these words would come to me: "I came unto my own, and my own received me not."

And yet, in time, you get to know the phonies almost at sight. As if you didn't have enough of your own, almost every new family that moved into St. Michael's in those days immediately ran to the rectory for help. In those cases, we checked with the parish they moved from, to see if they had been given relief there. A certain Mrs. Willoughby is a case in point. The moment she moved into St. Michael's, she arrived at the rectory door. She wanted assistance—money preferably. There was nothing humble about her attitude. She was aggressive and blunt. She said she had formerly lived in St. Bridget's Parish and that Monsignor Ryan had helped her. Now that she was in St. Michael's, she expected me to do as well. I gave her some assistance, and I wrote to Monsignor Ryan and asked if he had helped her.

He wrote back, "Yes, she has been helped by St. Bridget's, and it won't be her fault if she is not helped by St. Michael's." Later, I learned that most of her family, and its branches, had lived most of their lives on public and private charity.

Another case concerned a young Italian woman who lived on the top floor of a shabby flat in St. Lucy's Parish. Her husband was an immigrant weaver, and when he arrived in this country he could find no work. She came to me and begged me to help him. Her heartbreak was so real and her plea so fervent that, even though she resided outside the parish, I agreed to help.

I phoned Charles Van Hook, an engineer of the Watson Machine Company, and asked him to please try to find something for this young man to do. He phoned a hosiery concern, and an appointment was made to interview the immigrant. Everyone's hopes rose, and I was as elated as the young couple. It was easier than I had supposed. On the appointed day, I drove the man and his wife to the mill, in Paterson. We were treated most cordially, but the personnel director said that he was sorry, business was slack and they weren't hiring. Back we came to Jersey City, disappointed, and I promised to keep looking for employment for him. In the meantime, to keep them from despair, I gave them food and clothing.

One day the wife came in, and she was excited. She said that she had found a fruit-and-vegetable store for sale. It was on the corner of Fourth and Grove Streets, and if she could only buy it their troubles would be over. I became interested and figured that here was a bona fide case where it was a pleasure to help. I told her to bring me a record of receipts and expenditures at the store so that we could be sure that she was buying a business and not a lemon. She brought the figures, and it certainly looked like a going business to me.

To their inexpressible delight, I advanced this couple $250 with the understanding that they would pay back a little bit each week out of store receipts. They bought the store, and after one week of operation they brought $25 to me. I was amazed, because all my native caution warned me not to get involved with these people, and now my trust had proved that they were really of "the deserving poor."

The next week, they didn't show up, and I thought that business may have been poor. The following week I took a walk down to the store and found that it was closed up. They

162

had sold the stock and moved out. No one knew where. I went to their flat, and learned that they had checked out of there too. It isn't necessary to tell you that I never saw them again.

Another case concerned a young Negro. He was a stranger to me, but he was intelligent and had a fine speaking voice. He needed help badly, he said, and he couldn't seem to get a job because he was colored. I didn't ask him if he was a Catholic because, in a sense, we were concerned at the moment with holding the body together, not the soul. I gave him some money, and some food. After that, he became a "regular," showing up at the rectory with the same old speech, and always promising that the moment he got a job he would pay everything back. Each time he showed up, he got help.

Then one morning I received a phone call from him. I knew it was his voice the moment he said hello, but he said that he was an insurance agent and that my colored friend would lose his policy unless he paid his premium today. I felt sick. If only he understood that he didn't have to swindle me to get help! So I told the "insurance man" to please send my friend to the rectory, and I would give him enough money for the payment.

Then I phoned the second precinct and asked for two detectives at once. They arrived at once, too. When my colored friend showed up, the detectives were in the next room, with a door ajar, listening. They heard him ask for the money for his insurance, and they saw me pass it to him. Then they took him away, and a judge sent him to city jail. Within twenty-four hours his wife was in the rectory, beseeching clemency for her husband. Matters were bad enough before he went to jail, she said, but now they were infinitely worse. Would I please ask the judge to set him

163

free—please? She admitted that he had no insurance policy, that he had boasted of "conning" me into giving him money, but he would make restitution if only I'd have the authorities set him free. Within the next day or two, I received plea after plea from the young man. Well, after four days I figured that he had learned his lesson; so I arranged to have him set free. I never saw him again.

I am not embittered by any of this. It is all a part of the Way of the Cross, and a priest dares not presume to weed the bad ones from the good without some sort of proof. You only learn about the unworthy ones after you have helped. And if my young friend returned to the rectory right now, how do I know that this time he may not really need the help, that this time he may not really be looking for a job; that this time he may not be a thoroughly honest person who should not be turned away? How do I know? Frankly, I don't. In these situations, a priest may be a "sucker" twenty times in a row; but on the twenty-first time, he will have helped the right person, and for a moment the sun shines for the priest.

In the spring of 1932 St. Michael's High School held the first sodality seminar that had ever been held in the Diocese of Newark. We had sodalists from every Catholic high school in Jersey City. It began at ten in the morning, with a review of the fundamentals of organization. We had lunch at noon, and then the seminar was resumed in Public School 37, just a block away. There we heard from our young men and ladies in three-minute speeches on a variety of subjects:

1. What the sodality has done for our school.
2. Why we need leaders.
3. The committees we have organized and found worth while.

4. What we do at sodality meetings.
5. The student and Eucharistic devotion.
   Mass—Holy Communion—Guard of Honor—
   Frequent visits.
6. The student and Our Blessed Mother.
   Boys' point of view—Girls' point of view—Imitating Our Mother—Practices we have adopted to honor Her—The Respect Womanhood Campaign.
7. Our apostolic work in the school.
   Spreading literature—Learning to talk religion—Missions—Other forms of apostolic endeavor.
8. Literature and Publicity.
   Why we believe in Catholic literature—What are we doing to spread Catholic literature?—Is Catholic literature interesting?—Advertising methods as applied to our faith—Our bulletin board.

All of which must sound pretty dull in print, but I have a reason for telling it to you in detail. The average sodalist, reading it, must have yawned and said to himself or herself, "This is one meeting where I can catch up on my sleep." Anyone who said that was very much mistaken and did not reckon with Father Daniel A. Lord, S.J., director of the National Sodality, and Miss Dorothy Willman of the headquarters staff.

Father Lord knew that the first important thing is to capture the interest of the boys and girls. To do this he put on a skit called "The Flag and the Cross." It opens innocently enough, with a speaker discussing our duty to our country and our Church. But the orator had hardly uttered his first paragraph when two students ("plants") began to shift and squirm noisily, and they made some unkind references to the speaker. If you had been present, you would have seen how this upset the other sodalists. In a trice, nobody was sleeping. The two plants got up and began to bang their chairs around. The speaker, meanwhile, paused, and stumbled over words. The plants decided to leave, as loudly as possible, and one of them fell in the aisle. The speaker, at this point, stopped talking. At the same time, sixteen other plants in the audience added to the confusion by talking loudly among themselves, "Let the guy talk. . . ." "What happened . . . ?" "Give the speaker a break. . . ." "Who started this . . . ?" And only a girl would say this, "I never heard of such impertinence in my life!"

The speaker began to plead for order, but the hecklers grew greater in volume and number. Monsignor Griffin stood and ordered the disturbers to be quiet. This upset the entire audience because the Monsignor represented the voice of authority. Of course no one in the audience knew that even he was playing a "bit" part. Even the plants were hushed. That is, until they saw me beaming approvingly at their very realistic efforts. When it was explained to the audience that this was a matter of Catholic educational loyalty and a chance for a speaker to prove his poise under fire, everyone had a good laugh, including the Monsignor, and I assure you that the remaining speakers had no sleepers.

In June of 1932 I headed a pilgrimage to the Eucharistic Congress in Dublin. I had the approval of the Bishop and the Monsignor, and you can imagine how much this trip would mean to a second-generation Irishman who had heard stories, time and again, about the Ould Sod. I had heard of Wexford, Cork, Tipperary, Galway, and so many other places that, in my mind's eye, I had already been there; I knew the people and the places.

But one thing clouded the trip. My father had fallen gravely ill of a heart condition. In fact, up until the last moment, I was prepared to forgo the trip. But it was his urging, and the advice of his doctor, that changed my mind, and we sailed on the French liner *De Grasse*.

There were about fifty of us, and life on shipboard can be a fairyland. The food was fine, the conversation lively; the deck games were fun; and sleeping in the arms of a 20,000-ton mother who rocked you gently was indeed a pleasure. And all the way across the Atlantic, Monsignor Griffin radioed reports concerning my father, a most considerate act. Although at the start of the trip I was apprehensive, I felt more and more at ease as the reports continued to be more and more optimistic.

The first day in Dublin I saw Phoenix Park and got a good general view of the city. I had assumed that the faith of my people in St. Michael's was about as rich as faith can be, but in Dublin I found that the poor managed to set up little altars in their homes. I learned that one man sold his trousers to set up his altar. In Ireland the Church is part of everyday life and not merely reserved for Sundays and holydays of obligation. The church is on a level of importance with daily bread, and countless thousands attend Mass every morning of their lives and receive Communion too. But great as the faith was in Ireland, it taught me where the faith of the people of St. Michael's came from.

By a stroke of luck I ran into my brother, Father Raymond McWilliams, and, for a few hours, it was like old home week in Ireland. He had come over for the congress on a British liner, and it seemed wonderfully incongruous that we, two brothers who seldom saw each other in the United States, should meet on the far side of the Atlantic Ocean.

Then the joy died. A telegram came, and it said that my father had taken a turn for the worse, and that I'd better hurry right home. I boarded a little steamer for Liverpool at once and made connections with the French liner *Ile de France*, bound for New York. Father Raymond hurried to Queenstown and caught a Cunarder going home.

That trip was, for me, a sad one. My father was one of the greatest men I ever met, and this is not said because he was my father. The trip seemed endless, with day following night so slowly, and people enjoying themselves on deck and dancing to the tunes of an orchestra. To me, the trip was full of nostalgic thoughts; thoughts of better days; thoughts of boyhood; thoughts of a brother, somewhere out there on the same ocean, thinking the same thoughts and praying the same prayers.

When I landed, I had been to Ireland and back in two weeks. Father Raymond and I both got to Paterson in time. My father lived three days. A twenty-four-hour watch was kept over him. I was in the next room when the nurse stepped out of the sickroom for a moment. By the time she returned, my father had gone. He had lived a wonderful life, and he died in the arms of Jesus and Mary. That was the important thing.

My grief was secondary. It was the first death in my immediate family, and it taught me how one feels when someone so near and so dear passes on. I had been at hundreds of deathbeds and assisted at hundreds of funerals, but this taught me how the heart cries out, how much kindness and sympathy mean at a time like that, and how a priest can be loved by his flock in direct proportion to how close he comes to their lives in their sorrow. A priest might be a great philosopher and a brilliant theologian, but unless he can come down to the level of everyday living in a time of death, he will mean little to his parishioners. It seems awkward to say that a priest can learn something from the death of his own father, but I learned humaneness; I learned that the touch of a friendly hand on my shoulder was important; that a mumbled word means complete understanding; that a Hail Mary at the side of a casket can endear a stranger to you.

Monsignor Griffin was the soul of kindness throughout these days. He wanted to do everything to help, to ameliorate our grief, and he did. At the close of the Requiem Mass, he stood next to the casket and spoke beautifully over my father. Afterward, you never remember all the people you want to remember, but the Van Hooks, the Ryans, the Van Noorts, are families I can never forget.

Charles Van Hook was the executor of my father's estate, and with his high level of intelligence he set up the estate in such a way that all debts were faithfully discharged, and enough was left over for my mother to live out her life from a yearly income. She lived out her life alone, in the old family home, just as she wished it. She had friends, and she had sons to visit her often, but after father died, she wanted the peace of her own thoughts, and she had that peace.

As the Depression worsened, we opened a second cafeteria in St. Michael's. We opened this one for undernourished children, and, believe me, we had plenty of them. The WPA supplied a cook, waitresses, and a certain amount of food. Whatever else was needed was supplied by the parish. There was no charge, of course, for anything, and it would tear you wide open to see those little boys and girls, their eyes wide with hunger, lining up in an orderly and quiet queue, hoping that the soup and bread would be ready soon. Children, you may be sure, have more courage than adults. No matter how bad the hunger pains get, they will wait patiently, and they will smile as you pass by. It is the smile, I think, that breaks you down. They didn't ask to come here on earth; but, now that they are here, they cannot understand a world which will not feed them or clothe them. Uniformly they all think that their parents are the best in the world, even when they aren't.

The Doolans from Twelfth Street were people who should never have been permitted the care of children. They lacked character and about everything else that is good. But as is common to that breed, they had a raft of kids, and Mr. and Mrs. Doolan made a career of neglecting them. We fed all of them for a number of years.

The youngest child—a little boy—was a cripple, and when the mother and father went out, they chained him to a chair. He couldn't walk, but one day they must have forgotten to snap the lock securely, because he got loose. He crawled down the stairs, and crawled across Twelfth Street and all the way down the sidewalk of Erie Street until he got to Ninth. Then he crawled up Ninth, and by some intelligence which must be a gift from God he found his way to the basement of St. Michael's Church and to the cafeteria. When we tried to find out how he got there, he just pointed to the food. He wanted his lunch, that was all. There must be a special blessing on that baby because, besides being born a hopeless cripple, nobody ever loved him.

It was during this awful period that juvenile delinquency was on the rise, and this time a lot of Catholic boys were involved. In St. Michael's, it seemed to be concentrated in one block, and the police department's Bureau of Special Service knew every boy in that block but couldn't cope with the crimes they committed. Some of the things they did were pranks, rather than crimes. One day a fireman was walking home; and he didn't know it, but high in one of the tenements a boy had a bag full of juicy garbage, and he was drawing dead aim on the fireman. The kid had a good eye. He hit the fireman —plop!—right on the head, and the fireman tore the wet refuse from his face just in time to see a little head disappear. He was so mad that he flew up the stairs, but when he pounded on the door and explained what had happened the father of the boy withdrew his corncob from his mouth and said, "Now, you know that buys will be buys."

I went after the gang, but I got no more satisfaction than the fireman. I was rewarded with anonymous letters accusing me of being a Hitler, a Communist, and a few things that I'd rather not see in print. The gang was finally broken up, but it was a tragic end. One of the tenements caught fire, and two of the boys were burned to death. The gang broke up after that, and some of the families moved away, but now and then I read about the boys in the newspapers. One was recently arrested for a $1500 robbery in a packing plant. For this you can blame parents like the Doolans.

The Depression was pretty well behind us, in 1938, when we heard some good news. Monsignor Griffin had been in Washington for almost a week. He returned on a Friday evening, and except for greeting all of us he had nothing to say. About 9:30 the phone began to ring. It was the Associated Press, the United Press, and International News Service. They wanted some background on the new bishop, William A. Griffin. We were electrified. He had come home, and he hadn't said a word about the high honor which had been bestowed upon him by the Holy See. I was breathless as I supplied the pertinent facts about his life. When the Monsignor came downstairs the next morning, we were all waiting for him, and we told him that the news was out; and all of us offered our heartiest congratulations.

Any man in the priesthood who is promoted wins congratulations. But, in my time at least, I never heard anything like the universal acclaim which greeted the elevation of Monsignor Griffin. Chief Justice Thomas Brogan was almost lyrical.

"He's a man in a crowd!" he said. "He stands out in a group; there's something distinctive about him. No one more worthy could have received such an honor. In fact, it's the most comforting bit of news I've received in some time."

Without exaggeration it was the greatest honor ever to accrue to St. Michael's, and the people were thrilled to the marrow. We priests could hardly have been happier if it had happened to us. The whole Horseshoe got a great lift, and everyone seemed to vie with everyone else in trying to do honor to the new bishop and to present gifts.

I think that practically the whole parish journeyed to Newark, to sit in the unfinished Sacred Heart Cathedral to do him honor on the day of his consecration. They went in buses, in cars, and by train. It was a grand tribute to a most deserving priest, and it was not a thing that could be bought, or ordered.

Archbishop Thomas J. Walsh was the consecrator, and the day was May 1—the first day of the month of Mary. When it was over, and the new bishop, in his miter, walked back down the aisle distributing his blessing to the kneeling people, he looked every inch the part, and everyone felt that he would contribute greatly to the advancement of the Kingdom of God on earth.

The next big question, so far as St. Michael's was concerned, was, would Bishop Griffin stay on at St. Michael's or would he be assigned elsewhere? The doubt didn't stay with us long. Archbishop Walsh appointed him rector of the new Diocesan Seminary of Immaculate Conception at Darlington, New Jersey. I was made administrator of the parish again, and everyone sat back and wondered who the new pastor would be.

There are some practical truths about this question. We knew that, no matter who got the appointment, he couldn't be more spiritual than Monsignor Griffin or more appreciative than Father Corcoran. Thus, no matter whom we got, he would suffer by comparison with those two. On the other hand, I had been a priest twenty years and had never served in any parish but St. Michael's. Many of my classmates had been all over the diocese, and they were now being appointed to pastorates. I was due for an appointment as pastor of some parish—whatever parish it pleased His Excellency to send me.

Rumors ran through the parish that I was to be made pastor. Everyone knew the inside story, and told it freely. All of them knew about as much as I did—which was nothing. Credence was lent to these rumors when Bishop Griffin returned for a parish affair and in the course of his remarks said, "If you people pray hard enough, Father McWilliams might be the next pastor of St. Michael's Church." Psychologically, these rumors put me in a bad spot because now, if I wasn't appointed, in the eyes of my people it would almost amount to excommunication.

The miracle occurred on June 23, 1938, when I became the fifth irremovable pastor of St. Michael's. I still have the letter:

June 14th, 1938

Office of the Bishop

Rev. Leroy E. McWilliams
St. Michael's Rectory
252 Ninth Street
Jersey City, N. J.

Reverend dear Father McWilliams:

On May 9th I appointed you Administrator pro tempore of St. Michael's Church, Jersey City, N. J.

I now hereby name, constitute and appoint you Rector, Pastor, Parochum Amovibilem of St. Michael's Church in Jersey City, N. J. This appointment is effective Thursday, June 23, 1938, when after having made a profession of faith and taken the prescribed oath of office in accordance with Canon 1406, #7, on Friday June 17, 1938, at 11 A.M. before our chancellor, the Rev. Thomas A. Boland, you shall take possession hereunder. Kindly bring this letter with you at the required visit to the Chancery.

You shall read personally this letter at the principal Mass, and you shall read it, or have it read at all Masses in the Church of St. Michael, Jersey City, N. J., on Sunday, June 26, 1938 and file same in Parish archives thereafter.

Recommending you to the veneration, affection and co-operation of the noble people committed to your pastoral keeping and blessing the new Shepherd and his faithful flock, I am

Yours devotedly in Christ
Thomas Joseph Walsh
ARCHBISHOP OF NEWARK

174

Underneath, three days later, was written:

I hereby certify that the Rev. Leroy E. McWilliams made the profession of faith and oath directed in the above letter before me in the Chancery Office of the Diocese of Newark, 31 Mulberry Street, Newark, N. J. on the 17th day of June A.D. 1938 at 11:15 A.M.

Thomas A. Boland

CHANCELLOR

9

AND NOW the little altar boy of St. Joseph's in Paterson was the pastor of St. Michael's in Jersey City. I hoped that I would be a good pastor and that my priests and my people would regard me as a reasonable man. A letter went to the archbishop expressing appreciation for reposing so much confidence in me. I was forty-four, and I had given the best that was in me to my predecessors. I also realized that, in a sense, I had arrived too late because St. Michael's future was behind it. The church was seventy-one years old, and the grandeur and the people of its youth were gone. A debt of $68,000 didn't help matters much. Another important item was that I had two schools to maintain and administer. The overhead was high, and my first important duty was to step up the income of the parish.

The situation wasn't dismal, and it is not my intention to make you feel that it was. But I was now in a position of grave responsibility. The upkeep of the church, the schools, and the convent, and the daily existence of all the good sisters, depended upon me. The spiritual lives of thousands of persons were now in my hands. In many cases the daily livelihood and the food and clothing of parishioners were also my burden. It is an exultant feeling to reach the high estate of pastor of a church, but the moment it is attained the first ulcer begins to bud.

Of course hundreds of congratulatory telegrams and letters came to the rectory. If anything, they give the pastor a courage he might not have. What pleased me most, though, was the delight of Father Al Merity and Father Joseph Murphy, the two curates with whom I had worked for so long. They expressed themselves volubly and happily, and I knew that God had given me the grace of a head start in a new job. Together we would carry on God's holy work. With two such grand priests at my side, failure was out of the question.

Monsignor Bill Costelloe, now pastor of Holy Cross in Harrison, New Jersey, wired, CONGRATULATIONS. NOTHING HAS PLEASED ME MORE THAN THE NEWS OF YOUR APPOINT-MENT. BEST WISHES FOR THE NEW AND GREAT WORK I KNOW YOU WILL DO. My humorous classmate, Father Bernie Moore, wrote, "The thrill that comes once in a lifetime, to be able to spit on your own stove. Now that you are experiencing it, you have my heartiest congratulations. Take it easy, don't work too hard and live to enjoy it many years. I have hopes myself of joining the select circle in a couple of years. *Ora pro me*. Sincerely, Bernie."

Monsignor Thomas Burke, my next-door neighbor at St. Mary's, wrote, "The good news of your elevation to the pastorate of St. Michael's is confirmed in tonight's Jersey *Journal*. With your long residence there and your training under three excellent pastors, there is no doubt of your fitness or of your future success. . . ."

177

There were others. And all of them are now treasured keepsakes, to be studied when nostalgia creeps through the lonely heart. Monsignor Thomas F. Monaghan, of St. Paul's, wrote, "Accept my heartiest congratulations on the occasion of your much deserved promotion. May the good Lord bless you and prosper you always and crown with success your every effort for His honor and glory and for the salvation of souls. *Ad multos plurimosque annos.*" And one of the Monsignor's curates, Father Bill Buckley, an old friend, wrote, "Congratulations on your appointment as pastor of St. Michael's. Like that of Bishop Griffin, whom you succeed, I am sure your appointment is a most popular one. You have done a great job at St. Michael's for many years and may God give you the grace and strength to continue it *ad multos annos.*" Jimmy Crowe, a boy from St. Michael's, who died a Josephite priest, wrote, "You have been a model priest, a credit to your Bishop and now may you have good health and success."

The laity sent many fine messages. They came from the great and the small, and every one gave me a moral lift. Mayor Frank Hague wrote, "I am sure that no better choice could have been made and am sending this message as my assurance that I shall always respond cheerfully to any call you may make upon me to be helpful to my old parish." The other half of the famous team, Deputy Mayor John Malone, wrote, "I am sure everyone in St. Michael's Parish will join me in congratulating you upon your appointment as pastor. I shall always have a deep loyalty to St. Michael's and you must never hesitate to call upon me if I can be of service to you in its affairs." John Kenny, then Hague's lieutenant and the boss in the Horseshoe, wired, SINCERE GOOD WISHES UPON YOUR APPOINTMENT AS PASTOR AND I HOPE YOUR ADMINISTRATION WILL BE COMPLETELY SUCCESSFUL.

It is impossible to list them all. Each message meant something special to me, but would mean little to you. One other who was pleased with my appointment was Rita. Some time before, George Curran called me on the phone and asked me if I would like to have a dog. I had always loved dogs, but I hadn't had one of my own since grammar-school days.

So I said, "How big is it?"

He said, "About as big as you are."

I was tempted to say, "It must be a small dog," but, instead, I said, "What kind is it?"

"A black great Dane," he said.

At the time he called, I wasn't sure of my status in St. Michael's, and I hesitated a moment. But I love dogs so much that I took a chance. I said, "O.K., I'll take her."

And that's how I acquired Rita. We became pals at once. She was big, and she was as black as the inside of a derby hat, but she was loving and had an affectionate disposition. She would carry anything she could lift in her mouth, and she was an excellent watchdog. No soft footfall could ever get close to the rectory without Rita's rising out of sleep, ears cocked forward, and a low growl coming from deep within her throat.

I loved her and she loved me. It was a mutual affection which we both understood but never discussed. When I walked her, Rita was by my side whether I stopped to talk to someone, or whether I turned to walk in the opposite direction. She was quiet and faithful, and no one can ask more of an animal.

One morning, on my way to Mass, I took Rita outside and walked her around the block. When I returned, I left her to play outside the sacristy beside the church. I went up the steps, and she watched me as though she didn't understand why my duties would take me from her. I knelt in the sacristy in preparation for Mass, and in due time I vested and went out on the main altar for the parochial Mass. Everything about it was routine until near the end of the service. I turned around to give the last blessing when who appeared on the predella but Rita.

She had played for a while, but she must have worried some about what business would take me from her, and then she walked up the high iron steps leading to the sacristy, and, not finding me there, she used the wonderful nose that God gave her and sniffed her way to me on the high altar. When she approached, she wagged her tail, and, although I was in garments strange to her, she was happy. The sexton, Tom Murtagh, saw what had happened, and he came onto the altar surreptitiously and dragged Rita away. As soon as he released her, however, she bounded right back onto the altar, and when I moved over to the left side of the altar to recite St. John's Gospel, she moved over with me, and when I came down the steps for the foot prayers, Rita came down too, and finally she walked me back into the sacristy.

The following Sunday morning I met Barney Smith, an old-timer from Ireland with the wit that goes with it, and he said, "Say, Father, what kind of a dog is that you have? I've seen many of them, and they do some wonderful things, but this is the first time in my life I ever saw a dog assisting at Mass, alongside the priest on the top of the altar."

Rita and I were bosom friends for five years. And then, on an Easter Sunday morning, she died. We knew, the night before, that her life was ebbing, and we wrapped her tenderly in blankets and left her in a room off the kitchen. The next morning, when I arose, I found Rita, still alive, in the inner vestibule at the foot of the stairs. Even now, I cannot understand how, in her condition, she was able to drag herself through several rooms and doors to the spot where I found her. I knew what her intentions were. She wanted to come upstairs to reach my room, perhaps to say a mute farewell, a kiss of my hand. She died that day, and again I drank deeply of the cup of sorrow.

I have many fond memories of Rita. We were having a special dinner party in the rectory one time, and the cook baked a luscious chocolate layer cake. It reposed in all its beauty on the dining-room table. Somehow, Rita wandered in before the guests arrived, and she sniffed the layer cake, and it smelled good to her. Tentatively, she reached over and gave it a solid lick. It not only smelled good; it tasted good. And so, with her long and big neck, she went to work on the cake. She was still licking—not eating—when the cook walked in. I don't know what the cook did to her, but Rita ran for her life. Afterward the icing was smoothed over and fixed up so that not even a cake expert could tell that anything had happened. When the dinner was over, all the guests raved about the wonderful cake, and I sat there, gravely listening and thinking that it proves a lesson: what you don't know will never hurt you.

For a while, I was inconsolable. Still, time heals the wounds of the heart, and one day I was told that a family in Ridgewood had advertised great Dane puppies for sale. I drove up and was delighted to find that they were great dog lovers. There was a whole litter of fawn-colored baby Danes, a cat, a small beagle, and a hen called Butch. The chicken had been sterile for a long while and one day laid an egg. The family discovered that she had eaten dog food the day before.

One of the fawn pups, bigger than his brethren and with a black mask covering his face, took my eye and my heart. Of course—wouldn't you know?—I then discovered that this was the dog the family wanted to keep for themselves. However, I was just as determined as they, and finally they sold him to me. I named this one Michael, and in time he became the biggest and most famous dog in all the Horseshoe. Behavior was his strong suit. He chewed the dog mattress in the cellar, and he ate the laundress's shoes. He also liked to munch on chair coverings, and he had a weakness for turning the rugs back and eating the padding underneath. Not to do a disservice to Michael, I must tell you that all of this happened in the first year only. After that he was big and beige and dignified. He liked to ride in cars, until one day I inadvertently caught his tail in the door, and ever after he had to be coaxed into an automobile.

He was as fine a watchdog as Rita, even finer under analysis, because when Big Mike barked, the windows rattled in their casings, and a smart burglar could put a mile between him and Michael in four minutes flat. He always slept in my study, and at times when he had to go out he'd poke his long neck and head to where I was sleeping and tell me to get up and open the door.

Michael was one of the few dogs I knew who loved butter. He could walk around a dining-room table and expertly lick up every pat of butter in the place before the priests had finished washing up. And the worst part of it was that Michael never left any evidence. He did it one day, and a moment later when the cook returned to the dining room, she thought she must have forgotten the butter; so she took the plates back out into the kitchen and put more butter on. Michael waited in the hallway, as serene as an angel, until the cook returned to the kitchen. Then he bounded to his feet, made one round trip of the table, and all the butter was gone again.

This time the cook knew who the culprit was. So she refilled the little dishes and waited behind the kitchen door for the criminal to return to the scene of the crime. Sure enough

182

—Mike loped in prepared to make one more dash around the bases. But when he looked out of the corner of his eye and saw the cook racing toward him with a folded newspaper, Michael took off so fast that I really believe that none of his four feet touched the ground until he was safe in my study. The odd thing is that once he had been caught, he never did it again.

The strangest thing that happened in that rectory in all my years there was the night we were burglarized. The crime has never been solved, but it has so many strange aspects that it might be worth recounting. I was about to hear confessions in the church. The time was 7:30 P.M. By this time everybody in the area knew Michael, and everyone knew that he was bigger than a Crosley car and, in some ways, tougher. Therefore it can be assumed that no neighborhood burglar would dare take a chance in the rectory.

On that particular night I did something that I never did before. I locked Mike up in the downstairs study, which is in the front of the rectory. I had a reason for this: we had just employed a new maid, and I was afraid that the dog would frighten her. Still, I told no one that the big fellow was locked in the study, and no one saw me do it.

I walked into the church and heard confessions until nine. Then I returned to the rectory and went immediately to my study, which is on the second floor front. To my amazement, everything was thrown on my desk and around it. The middle drawer had been jimmied. I phoned the police, and in a few minutes a police captain and three detectives were there. I summoned the sexton and the two curates, who hurried to their rooms and learned that they too had been robbed. The crook was particular—he ignored rolls of coins and took only bills.

The officers of the law were not too helpful. They couldn't

183

find out how the burglar got into the rectory, nor did they seem to want to take fingerprints. Five days later, at my insistence, a fingerprint expert arrived, but all he got were faint smudges.

The first real discovery was made by a part-time worker, Helen Johnson, who was cleaning Father Merity's room in the rear of the second floor when she noticed the clear marks of a man's hand on the bedroom wall and on the window sill. Outside that window was the roof of our sun porch, and there, outlined in mud, were a man's footprints. The same footprints were found on the ground below.

It became clear to all of us how the burglar had pulled the job. And the burglar must have known that we priests would be hearing confessions at that time. But he couldn't have known about Michael's being locked up, and if the burglar knew enough about the layout of the rectory to burgle it without blundering, then he must have known that we had a big dog. And this in turn leads to the conclusion that he and Mike were friends.

Standing in the areaway between the rectory and the church, we could see how the job had been pulled. He had gone up the three steps leading to the sun porch, had reached up to the high sill above, and by shinnying against the wooden wall had managed to get a purchase on the roof above and then hoisted himself up. It was quite a feat of climbing, and whoever did it was an expert.

Directly opposite the sun porch was the girls' dining room, and at the time of the theft the cook sat there with the radio blaring. When the employment agency first sent her to me, I asked if she was an old lady and they said, "Oh, no, Father. Not old!" I later learned that she was eighty-five years of age, and now I'd like to know, "How old is old?" Although the burglar was outside her window, she could not hear him with that radio blasting in all directions. When I questioned her about it, she shrugged and seemed to be completely indifferent; so—God forgive me—I began to suspect her.

The following day we saw the old cook go out with a brown package under her arm. To me it looked like a package of bills. We made her number one on our Police Hit Parade for the following morning. But, under questioning, she said that she had taken the remainder of a meat loaf from the refrigerator, wrapped it up, and taken it to a friend whom she visited in Coney Island. As a detective, I turned out to be a pretty fair priest.

By a process of elimination I learned that it could not have been the new maid, because she left the house early. The only others who might have done the job were the painters, who had been doing over all the rooms for three weeks. We investigated the painters quietly and learned that one of them had been a steeple jack. We also learned that he was heavily in debt and owed some back rent. A detective shadowed this man for months, but he never spent more than a dollar in a saloon and he never tried to pay the back rent that he owed. Besides, I remembered that all the painters were mortally afraid of Michael, and they wouldn't work unless he was tied up.

When I locked Michael in the study, it was a last-minute decision on my part. And if the robbery was perpetrated by a complete stranger who didn't know we had a dog, then how did he go directly to my desk and jimmy the middle drawer when the truth is that, until shortly before the burglary, I had never kept money in this desk? Nothing else in the room was disturbed, and the steel safe—which would be the logical target for a thief—was on the first floor.

A year later one of the detectives stopped at the rectory to tell me that there was no mystery about the robbery, except in my mind. The thief was the steeple-jack painter, but it would be no use arresting him because he had never tried to spend any of the money and, if we couldn't convict him, he could sue me for false arrest. Still, even the theft had a good purpose. It showed the loyalty of my people, all of whom fell over each other trying to help me.

I never locked Michael up again, and we had some great times together. When I left the rectory and couldn't take him with me, he waited silently and patiently at the door, and the moment he heard my footfall outside his big brown tail would start to beat the rectory floor. When I took him out, his face lit up as though I had just handed him a million. And yet it took so little to please him, and he gave so much affection and loyalty in return until his death at my cabin in Highland Lakes in 1950.

For a while, I thought of buying another Dane—I knew that I'd never be completely happy without a dog—but then I felt that there was only one Michael, and I began to think of other breeds of dogs. It was Guy Manning, executive director of the Jersey City Community Fund, who interested me in Irish setters. He and his wife "Joe" had raised them, and Guy assured me that if I got a good setter, he'd "do anything but write your sermons for you."

I was still sorrowing, but, like the new widow, I was also looking. One of the things I looked at was a book called *The Care and Training of Dogs*, by Arthur Frederick Jones, who was also the editor of *The American Kennel Gazette*, and what he wrote about Irish setters settled the matter.

". . . Few are so like the people of their native lands as is this red-coat from Erin—or Eire if you insist. Not even the British bulldog is more typical of the citizens of the country from which he came. In sharp contrast to many other bird dog breeds, he's usually as bold as a lion, and, while not spoil-

186

ing for a fight, is not averse to 'a bit of a shindy' when the occasion requires. Yet no dog living has greater charm, more of 'a way with him,' or can turn on the blarney with more telling effect. Surely no other bird dog has both his devil-may-care disposition and his likable and even lovable disposition as well. . . . Physically, he's a picture, as strikingly handsome as they come. That stunning mahogany coat of his catches the eye at a glance. . . . We defy any draftsman to reduce the Irish setter to a mere blue print, for he has qualities that just don't lend themselves to any ordinary mold."

Eventually, I got Pooh, a champion Irish setter, from Kate Smith. She is one dog breeder who has a genuine love of animals and fine business integrity. The first one she sent, Bryan, caught pneumonia and died, so she sent Pooh to replace him. I was curious about his name, and Miss Smith told me that Pooh's father was Christopher Robin. The family who owned him had a little boy to whom had been read A. A. Milne's book *Winnie the Pooh*. The boy was so fond of the youngster in the book, Christopher Robin, that the dog was named after him. And when Mr. Robin became a father, all the pups were named after other characters in the book. That's how Pooh got his name, and he's as regal and friendly as any dog I've ever seen.

10

Two THINGS happen at once to a new pastor. First, he is lost in a brilliant blizzard of congratulations. Second, he often finds himself in a fog of debt. It happened that way to me, and the elation of promotion was quickly replaced by the frown of worry. I had heavy obligations and, like most newly created pastors, I also had plans to improve my church. Moreover, the parish income was going downhill—slowly, to be sure—but downhill just the same.

In the east transept of the church was a walnut console from which the main organ, as well as the chancel organ, could be played. This console we seldom used, so I sold it back to the Skinner Organ Company and received a neat little check that started us back on the road to solvency. The next thing I did was to lay the foundations for a suit against the Erie Railroad for smoke and soot damage to the church and other buildings. When Mayor Frank Hague heard about it, he ordered his lawyer, Charles Hirshenstein, to help us in any way possible. As a result, years later the railroad settled out of court for $2500. I hope that the fact that Hague could have enacted crippling ordinances against the railroad had nothing to do with the settlement.

However, without the help of the people of St. Michael's, the continued, unremitting help, the rest of it would have meant nothing. I appealed to the people, and the people responded. They were wonderful. They not only gave and gave and gave, but they thought up new ideas for raising more money. In one year we were able to clean and repaint the church from vestibule to sacristy, redecorate the auditorium, and purchase new chairs. We relocated the baptistery in the west vestibule and set up a shrine to Our Sorrowful Mother. The west transept of the church was transformed into Our Lady's Chapel and was made the nucleus of a shrine to Our Lady of the Miraculous Medal. A rich oriental rug was bought for the sanctuary, and new vestments, made in Europe's oldest houses, were added to our wardrobes. Two new classes were opened in the high school, and the kindergarten of the elementary school was relocated in the first grade. A weekly novena was started to Our Sorrowful Mother in August, 1939, and attracted 1200 people every Friday. In October I started a regular weekly religious broadcast over Station WAAT, the first in the history of the archdiocese. A gummed rubber kneeler, with dark-red velours covering, was installed before the sanctuary rail and also in front of the Sorrowful Mother shrine. Three oil paintings were added to the shrine, and in the alcove on the other side of the church we installed a full-length portrait of the Master knocking on the door. The Via Matris was also put up over the Stations of the Cross. They were reproductions, in oil, of Janssens' original work in the cathedral at Antwerp. In that same summer of the first year the front of the church was repainted, and a landscape artist fixed up the grounds.

And yet, in spite of all this, I was happy to be able to report to my people, at the expiration of eighteen months, that the total parish debt was now down to $60,500 and in two months would be further reduced to $58,000.

At the end of 1940 I wrote: "Our receipts for last year amounted to $89,000, an increase over last year of $7,000. Our expenditures, however, amounted to $85,000. The increase is mainly due to increased enrollment in the high school and the increased number of people who attend parish parties. It is through this extraparochial activity that we have made up for diminishing Christmas and Easter and regular Sunday and monthly collections. No one knows better than we do of the many who have died and the many more who have moved away. No one is more acutely aware than we of how sections of the parish have gone down and depreciated. . . . The point we have been making is that we have managed to keep up the old standards and have established new ones. We have maintained a healthy life and vigor in the face of greatly changed conditions in lower Jersey City."

I listed the improvements: four in the convent, ten in the church, three in the school. One item was the acquisition of the entire exhibit of Grosse & Company religious vestments in the Belgian Building at the World's Fair. When the fair was over, I wondered if the company planned to take all the vestments back to Bruges. I was delighted to find that they would sell, and sell at a most reasonable price. It was a gorgeous collection and gave St. Michael's as fine a set of vestments as you will find anywhere in the United States.

In that same issue of *The Parish Bulletin*, I wrote: "No man could be pastor of this parish without recognizing the invaluable services rendered by John Kenny. A successful businessman, prominent and able in public life, he yet remains an humble and exemplary member of this parish. His talents, his influence and prestige he unfailingly places at the disposal of his Church for the greater glory of God and the good of his fellow man. The number of those whom he has helped are legion, and only on the last day at the Great Assize will his many charities be known. We can testify that, privately, he has come to us and left substantial donations for the poor. These things are not written in the public ledger, but they are recorded in the Book of Life.

"He is the only political leader in the city that we know of, that sponsors and exclusively manages a gigantic entertainment for the poor of his parish. It is tops among things of its kind. . . ."

I did not know then that someday Mayor Frank Hague would fight to the political death with his protégé, John Kenny, and that Kenny would win and become mayor of Jersey City. I do not use a crystal ball when I write.

The war came along, and in 1942 the boys of St. Michael's began to leave. The size of our honor roll grew and grew until, at length, 650 names were on it. Every week scores of worried mothers and fathers and sisters and brothers would come to the altar rail to kneel and to pray and to light the big seven-day candles which kept alive their prayer and petition before the Lord.

With war comes prosperity. Man thrives on his own cruelty, and soon everyone who was home was working. Men who had held up a wall on the street corners for years had jobs. Many of the women of the parish were working, too. Economically, St. Michael's people never had it so good. The money was rolling in from everywhere, and new linoleum was being hammered down in the kitchens, and the old radio was dropped into the ash can to be replaced by a newer, bigger one, with record-playing attachment. The ladies had new hats and new dresses, and Pop sported new shoes and a new suit. Everybody could afford to go to the movies two or three times a week, and boys just out of high school were making more money than my father did when he built his own house. There weren't many cars to be bought, and gasoline was rationed, but the people of St. Michael's got their share of luxury, and many who had walked the two or three blocks to the church all their lives now rode.

Spiritually, the parish was as good as before, if not better. The priests redoubled their efforts to quicken the devotion of the people and to bring souls back to God. The parish income zoomed to $100,000, but expenses were $99,000. The high school was further expanded, and a new fluorescent-lighting system was installed in the church and in the auditorium. If the interior of the church was being beautified, it was important to permit the people to see it. Besides, fluorescent lighting cut our electric bill in half.

Sometimes, out of a problem comes a small miracle. We had invested some money in stainless-steel ware for the cafeteria in the basement of the church, but we couldn't find any place to keep it. It was by no means a distressing problem, but it came to the attention of Mrs. Frank Sheridan, one of our tireless women workers. She is the mother of Father Frank Sheridan, and, by a former marriage, also the mother of Hudson County Supervisor Bernard Hartnett. Mrs. Sheridan said that she knew a man named John Tiedemann, who was handy with tools, and that Mr. Tiedemann could make a chest to hold "all the silver."

I met John and gave him the job. Well, now, when that chest was completed, I took one look and I recognized the hand of the true artisan, the rare artisan. It was beautiful and it was sturdy. So I gave him some more tasks to do. They were accomplished so expertly that I offered John permanent employment at St. Michael's. He accepted the job, and in the next ten years the things we accomplished together are hardly short of fantastic. Only another pastor will realize how lucky I was to get John Tiedemann. He is the Michelangelo of the tool chest, and what he has done for our church and our schools—the entire plant, in fact—is a permanent tribute to the hand and eye God gave him.

Before he came to work for me, John was an independent contractor and, for that matter, still is. He drove around in an old secondhand, half-ton Chevvie truck, and he picked up jobs wherever he could find them. His skill was phenomenal, and the only thing he lacked was an administrative partner. I assumed that job, and we became a remarkable partnership.

He is a taciturn man, and he cares little about money. Add to this the fact that he is married and has ten children, and you begin to realize how badly he needed a hardheaded partner who would make sure that people paid him adequately.

John had hardly started to work in St. Michael's when he met Billy Connors. Bill was a shy grammar-school kid who wouldn't say beans if you begged him. But he felt a fierce devotion to John's work, and every afternoon after school Billy could be found in the basement workshop with John. Little by little he learned about tools and how to use them. John taught the boy the high standard of painstaking craftsmanship he used himself, and all through his high-school days, Billy worked with John, silently and well. Then Billy Connors' mother died, and John, with ten children of his own, took Billy Connors into his household as one more son. The two continued to work together, and Billy grew up to be a fine craftsman. He married John's niece, and in a year they had a bouncing baby girl. A few years ago, I appointed Billy as sexton of the church.

So you can see what happened when I couldn't find a place to put the stainless steel.

But the value of John Tiedemann to St. Michael's can never be measured in dollars and cents. He has solved problems which have baffled competent engineers. And yet John never graduated from grade school. He didn't like school, and he left before anyone could have handed him a degree for "savvy." Savvy is difficult to define, but John has it in enormous quantities. It is an inherent ability to understand a situation quickly, and to reason it out. For instance, my predecessors had difficulty with water in the basement of the church. In fact, the entire parish has the same trouble. When the sewers were put in the Horseshoe, almost a century ago, they were too small-throated to handle a heavy rain, and the water thereupon backed up into the cellars. Bishop Griffin, like his predecessors, sought professional advice and was told to install electric sumps. It was, they told him, the only answer. The sumps were installed. But they were effective only when the water reached them, and I have known occasions when the water went right on past the sumps without anything happening. We still had water in the basement.

I asked John to look the situation over. He did. He studied it from inside the church and outside. It didn't take him long. When he returned, he suggested that we put large valves on the sewer mains which flanked the church. Each of these valves would have an iron lid which would flap into a closed position the moment water started to back up toward the church. In other words, as long as water was outward bound, toward the street, the valves would remain open, but if the barest trickle started the other way, the iron lid would slam closed, stopping the water. I told him to proceed with the job. John picked up the valves in a secondhand shop for

$12.50 apiece, and installed them. We never had a bit of trouble with water again.

Fluorescent lighting was new when John installed ours. When I gave him the O.K. to put them in, he studied the job for a few minutes and then said he was sure that we could use the tops and bottoms of the beautiful Italian chandeliers then in use. We finally settled on a hanging, cylindrical fixture covered with panes of amber-tinted glass. John took care of installing the fixtures, and we experimented with various-sized fluorescent tubes until we found exactly the right one. After it was finished, it caused so much discussion that architects came from all over to see it in operation with the idea of introducing it in other churches.

What didn't that man do for us! We built five new classrooms and a faculty room in the high school. The work was all laid out by John and executed by him and his helpers. He completely overhauled the heating system in the convent and put in a new boiler and oil burner. He installed three oil burners in the church and school and the rectory, and he also kept them in repair. When it became necessary to insulate the roofs of the school, the sacristy, and the rectory, John did the job with the help of one or two of his children.

Probably the biggest recurring headache was the basement of the church. Here was our auditorium, a huge place with concrete floor and pillars, and old brick walls which were always damp. We could paint those walls every sixty days, and still the paint would peel. My predecessors must have, many a time, thrown up their hands in despair. Unfortunately, they didn't have John Tiedemann; and I did. As fast as John performed the miracles, I called for more; so, one day when he had no fresh ones to perform, he and I journeyed down to the auditorium and looked it over. John rubbed his hands against the moist walls, and he smelled it.

Then he said he'd see what could be done, and he left for New York.

When he returned, the problem was solved. He brought back a sample of a material called Marlite, a baked plastic with a backing of Masonite. It was as hard a substance as you can imagine, and we ordered quantities of it in smooth coral and beige. But, first, John put fir stripping down the old wall. Then he put the new wall on top of it. This provided an air space between the two walls and gave the old basement the ventilation it needed to absorb the dampness The old windows, with semicircular tops, were changed in shape and size, and every other one of these old windows was covered by the new wall. He and Billy Connors transformed that old auditorium so that, when the parishioners first went downstairs when it was finished, they couldn't believe their eyes. We never have trouble with dampness, and the Marlite can be kept clean with a cloth. The Marlite people took a look at it and sent photographers over to make pictures.

The next item of importance was a new cafeteria. This too is located in the auditorium. For ten years we had been feeding 300 school children a day at an old, secondhand cafeteria, and it was time that we got a new one. Again I talked it over with John, and again he came up with the answers. He laid out the idea for a modern stainless-steel cafeteria and kitchen, a curved soda bar, and a juke box for music. Bids were received from different firms, and the best one came from Onori & Sons, of Hoboken. John worked closely with them, and when the job was finished, the new cafeteria became the "rave" of the city. Today we can cook and serve any kind of meal in the cafeteria, and we can take care of large numbers of people. When school is in session, we have one woman who takes care of all the cooking, and three women volunteers who help serve the students. Two nuns are in charge of operations, and they are assisted by some students.

Everything was now completed in the auditorium except two items. One was rest rooms. We needed two, and John had them built of tile. The other was a refreshment bar. We had an old one, but it wasn't in keeping with the grandeur of all our new appurtenances. We got a bid on a new one—$800. It was too much, so John went out, bought some mahogany, and, with the aid of some friends of his, built as nice a bar as you ever saw. He finished it in such a way that it is impervious to stain and maintains its natural, light brown color. Total cost: $200.

A few years later, when Sister Grace Antonia was appointed superior of the convent, one of her first requests was for a chapel in the convent. We have twenty-four sisters, which is quite a few. One, Sister Christopher, has been with us forty-four years. All of them do so much and ask for so little, that, even though we couldn't afford a chapel, I made up my mind that, somehow or other, it would be built.

Since 1916 the sisters had used an enclosed bridge between the second floor of the convent and the choir of the church for daily devotions. In going back over the old records I found that each new sister superior had asked for a convent chapel, but nothing had ever been done about it. To make matters worse, most of the other convents in the archdiocese had chapels of their own. Having God residing in the convent all the time gives a different feeling to life within those walls.

Mother Grace Antonia said that the sisters did not hope for much of a chapel, but, whatever it was, they would be most grateful for it. Of course the first step was to call John in for a consultation. I had given him a copy of Dom Roulin's classic work, *Modern Church Architecture*, and he had familiarized himself with it. Together we toured the convent, and we decided that the best location for the chapel would be the recreation room on the first floor. It was big, and it had a bay window facing on the back of the convent. It also had a beveled wooden ceiling with oak wainscoting on the walls. It was connected with a smaller room, in front, by a simple arch. The more we looked at it, the more we decided that this room was a natural.

I also made another decision at the same time: I would not sponsor a makeshift chapel. If the sisters were to get one, then let it be a good one. Further, if we used this room, we would have to create another community room on the second floor, and that, in turn, meant tearing down five private rooms. This, in turn, meant setting up five private rooms somewhere else in the house. Also, we'd have to build a sacristy. The longer I looked at this problem, the bigger it became. To build a chapel, it began to look as though we'd have to tear the convent down.

John and I made trips to many other convents to study their chapels, and I finally decided that the convent needed major renovations anyway; so what started out as a simple chapel soon became a major work. We consulted with an architect, and when the plans were finished they were submitted to the building committee of the archdiocese and approved.

Soon the unearthly quiet of the convent was filled with the sounds of hammers and whirring electric saws and the heavy tramping of carpenters. John laid the wooden flooring and built a stately, but simple, altar of oak. He removed the arch separating the rooms and continued the scheme of wood beveling along the ceiling and the oak wainscoting on the walls. He broke through the back wall and provided an entrance into what had been a bedroom, but would now be the new sacristy. For many months John and shy Billy Con-

198

nors worked, and then the main work was completed. We called in Otto Theys, the painter, and worked out a combination of blue and gold for ceiling and side walls; and when it was finished it looked beautiful. Over the altar we erected a canopy of rich coverings which made the altar stand out above all else in the chapel. The backdrop was of fluted red velvet on which were mounted orphreys of black and gold and blue. Inside the canopy was a sunburst with a dove in the center on gold satin, with golden rays streaming out to the sides. The pews were of solid walnut, so that, standing to the rear, you got the impression of being in a small, beautifully designed church.

What John had wrought was terrific. Years later, when I invited a writer friend of mine to look at it, he said that he felt a constriction in his throat that no cathedral had ever induced.

When John finished, we still had a job to do. I had to go to our good people and ask for the furnishings. We asked, and we received. Among the items donated were a bronze tabernacle and candlesticks, a gold chalice, pyx and ciborium, opalescent windows, and the walnut pews, small, hand-carved wooden Stations of the Cross and a credence table, a sanctuary lamp, missal and missal stand, gold-filled Communion patens, and an altar rail of hand-hammered Swedish wrought iron, vestments and a vestment case, a stainless-steel sacrarium and gold plate with cruets, and many other things. The man who donated the chalice did so in memory of his little boy, whom he had accidentally killed with an old musket when they were playing cops and robbers. He knew that every time the chalice was raised his son would be remembered, and from that thought he and his grieving wife received great consolation.

Altogether, the chapel and the furnishings came to about

$10,000. If you could have stood with me the morning the good sisters got their first look at it, you would have said that it was worth ten million. Those shining faces; those trembling fingers; the look of love at this, their own, is something difficult to commit to paper. They thanked me, but it was my partner who did the work. If it hadn't been for John, the cost would have come to at least $20,000, and that would have been impossible.

Still, John's magnum opus lay ahead of him. It was to come in 1951 when St. Michael's gymnasium and high-school annex were created under his supervision. They are both substantial fireproof buildings, and the gymnasium can be pitted against any other in the city.

This project came about when two inspectors for the State Board of Education made an unannounced visit to St. Michael's in the spring of 1950. They inspected and inspected, and on the basis of their report the state again approved our high school for only one year and gave us eighteen months in which to build a gymnasium. Up to this time, we had been using the gymnasium of P.S. 37, a block away, plus a large playground directly across the street, and our own auditorium in bad weather. However, all these together did not satisfy the state board, and so the pressure was applied.

I blew up. Each student had only 150 minutes a week to put in on physical education, and one of these periods may be purely instructional. I don't know whether St. Michael himself was out to get these two inspectors; but, a few months later, one of them dropped dead behind the wheel of his automobile, and the other was transferred to another job. Still, their personal tragedies did not improve the position of our school. For months I tried to figure out how we could comply with the state order, and still not incur an impossible debt. All my philosophical teachings have proved that man cannot worry a problem into solution. Time and prayer and a calm approach are the best weapons, but this one harassed me so much that I could think of little else.

Then the solution came. Just like that. In the autumn of 1950 I heard that a building on Florence and Bright Streets had to come down to make way for a new housing project. The building had been put up, in 1941, by the Federal government. The junk dealers had already put in bids on the dismantling of the building when I first heard about it. I hurried to Mayor John Kenny, and he and Director of Public Safety Messano were most cooperative. Deputy Tax Collector William Black was advised to explore the entire matter, and, after two months of investigation, he came up with a report which showed (1) that the city could not sell the property; (2) that ownership of the property reverted to the Federal government unless it was used for educational purposes; (3) that the city could donate the building to an educational institution.

Thank God for friends in City Hall! At a meeting of the city commission, it was voted to donate the building to St. Michael's High School, on condition that St. Michael's dismantle and re-erect the building at its own expense. Now what had I been worrying about all those months? How ridiculous it seems now. In its own good time the solution came, and I fell to my knees with thankfulness.

This meant that the old partnership was in business again, and John and I examined the building and the property like construction experts. He had a friend named Al Bubas who had a 1924 truck with a derrick on it. The friend also owned a thirty-five-year-old Iron Horse, a portable hoist with big iron wheels. Al was the soul of generosity. He asked only a dollar an hour for the use of the equipment when in use, nothing at all when not in use. Another friend of John's, named Steve Strall, was hired, and then, with Billy Connors, my crew began to dismantle the building. A junkman told me that in his bid for pulling the thing down he had specified a period of three months. John had it down in three weeks and also had it transferred to St. Michael's property. This also included a Koven Water-film Boiler, oil burner, pipes, and blowers. This equipment was only two years old, as good as new. My boys marked everything with numbers and symbols, so that there was no confusion at all when they began the job of reassembling and rebuilding.

My original intention was to spend about $25,000 and rebuild the structure exactly as it had been, with corrugated metal roof and siding. But after the foundation and concrete floor had been laid, and we had raised the height of the building from 12 feet to 20, I decided we'd better put on a strong wooden roof and a brick front. It was an added expense, but it meant a much better-looking building and a more permanent one. As the work went on, we decided that a balcony would look nice, also a modern kitchen, a combination cloak and meeting room, and a ticket office.

Here we were again—off to the races. Then I decided to go the whole hog on the locker room and dressing rooms and on completely tiled showers. When it was finished, we plastered the walls from floor to ceiling and covered the concrete floor with asphalt tile. Ah, it was beautiful. We now had a building, adjoining the high school and connected to it, 56 feet wide and 115 feet long, capable of seating 1000 people. It would never have to apologize to any other gymnasium, and, once again, it was John's handiwork.

When we first assumed the job, "Bus" Clarke, a city engineer, had his doubts. When it was finished, he looked at it and grinned. "All I can say," he said, "is that you certainly got the right man." Bernard Berry, president of the

Jersey City Board of Education, came down to have a look, and he said it was a marvel of economy, planning, and workmanship.

I was sitting back congratulating myself and feeling very good indeed when the sister principal came to me and said that we needed four more classrooms and they'd have to be ready by September. I almost fell. Four more classrooms? Four at the rate of between $30,000 and $40,000 a room? I was in no mood to think of more construction, and more indebtedness. My head was spinning with dollar signs. When would it ever stop?

But, here again, my hand was forced. Our enrollment was up; the students had to have room in which to study and work; we had torn down one classroom which had jutted in the direction of our brand-new gymnasium; and now I could see St. Michael standing in front of a pawnbroker's office. This was the end. It would cost at least $120,000—a bare minimum of $120,000—and where would it ever come from in a parish that was supposed to be on its deathbed?

I went into executive session with John, and he went over the cost of masonry and materials with a contractor named Schultz. In September His Excellency, the Most Reverend James A. McNulty, Auxiliary Bishop of Newark, blessed the new annex. It was finished; it was fireproofed, and it had been approved. We had four new classrooms—four *elegant* classrooms—with aluminum frames and windows. And do you know what, my friends? The total cost under John's supervision, was $25,000. I don't blame you—I can't believe it myself!

By this time John was my pet story to tell. I attended a luncheon meeting of the American Cancer Society at the Plaza Hotel, and I was exchanging small talk with Postmaster Billy Kern, Dr. Vincent Butler, Bernard Berry, Pastor Ed

Grubb, and others, when Berry brought up the subject of the new gymnasium and how capable John was. That was all I needed. I started to talk about John and of the mighty things he had done for St. Michael's, and they all listened with polite credence until I told them the story of the lake.

I had brought John and Billy Connors up to the lake with me one summer. Near my cabin the water was full of submerged tree stumps, dangerous to swimmers and to sailboats. John said that he could get the stumps out, but I said it was impossible because to do so would mean staying under water for long stretches. John and Billy went back to town and bought a diving suit from the Surplus Commodities Commission and brought this back with an electric beer pump. John got into the diving suit, and Billy manned this air pump. Before that day was over several tree stumps were loosened, and later hauled on shore by a truck equipped with block and tackle.

I was amazed, when I finished the story, to find that my audience was guffawing insanely and emitting Bronx cheers of disbelief. Nothing I could say would make these eminent gentlemen believe that my John could do such a thing. But he did. And I saw it.

In the early days of the war my activities began to branch out beyond the parish. I had always believed that a priest should take an interest in the community life and should, if he can be of assistance, become a part of it. If such activity means the neglect of his duty to his church, of course he should not try to undertake anything else because, in so doing, he loses in all directions. But I had always had a lively interest in the world outside St. Michael's, and when, during the war, I was offered an appointment to the Price and Rationing Board, I accepted at once. The chairman of the board was M. Lester Lynch, who had been directly appointed by James Kerney, state OPA director. Mr. Lynch put me in charge of fuel oil, and it was a bewildering assignment at best.

The autumn of 1942 and the winter of 1942–1943 were inordinately cold. The government had based the oil quotas upon normal weather, and the allowances were far from sufficient to keep homes heated. All of us on the board were equipped with loose-leaf books so that as the new daily directives arrived we could add them. The government asked us to push conversion from oil to coal as vigorously as possible. We did. And then, suddenly, we were asked to reverse our field and push conversion from coal back to oil. I tried to be fair, but I soon learned, in dealing with the general public, that justice is not what they want. They want special privilege, and anything less than that brings wrath on the head of the administrator.

Still, it was good experience for me. I was dealing with non-Catholics as well as Catholics, and I know that some of the "nons" were surprised to find that, under the cassock, the priest is a friendly human being. Some seemed surprised that I could laugh or tell a joke. Others seemed a little startled that I did not hold my hands in an attitude of perpetual prayer. Still others, I am certain, expected to see horns and a tail. But mostly, they were surprised, I guess, because I devoted time to my job and wanted to see it through.

For the next two years I was in charge of the food panel, and I liked this job much better because it put me in contact with so many wholesalers and retailers and restaurateurs. The government regulations changed so often that I felt like an acrobat. Whenever I had matters running fairly smoothly, a new OPA regulation tossed the program right out the window.

I enjoyed meeting so many people because I like people—

all kinds of people. On the panel we had every race, creed, and nationality I had ever heard of. To them I was the Church in miniature, and their estimation of the Church rose or fell depending on whether I executed my tasks wisely or stupidly. Among them were real noblemen and noble-women, not of my faith, and they worked hard to help the war effort. There were no differences of opinion which could not, and were not, settled by honest talks across the table.

Two persons I cannot forget were Audry Ferrara, who was assigned as secretary to me, and Anne Tandler. Audry was, by coincidence, a Catholic. She was indefatigable. Anne, who was secretary to the chairman, Lester Lynch, was Jewish. She was as intelligent a girl as I've met, real to the core, and she had an almost global knowledge of what rationing was all about. Any board member who found himself perplexed about something had only to drop in to see Anne Tandler, and in a trice he understood the problem and was well on the road to solving it.

The sooner that we gentlemen of the cloth realize that an old era has died and that a new one has taken its place, the better off we'll be. Too many people are outside our faith, groping for answers. Too many people fear the Church in its ever-growing numbers. A priestly priest who will concern himself with the problems of his community and is willing to become a party to their solution does an excellent public-relations job, and by his example shows to others that the Church is a great house of mercy and understanding. As the editor of *The Catholic World* once wrote: "Eventually, why not now? We are a minority with a role to play, not a battle to fight."

It is my opinion that M. Lester Lynch, as chairman of the board, performed an outstanding work. He took a lot of nothing and made it into a lot of something. However, I feel that we may have stepped on some important toes by withholding "C" gasoline ration books. At any rate, Hague wanted a new chairman, and coincidentally after a conference of Judge Fake and other Federal judges, Lester was offered the post of United States Commissioner. He accepted, and immediately orders were issued for a testimonial dinner to him.

In Jersey City there are wheels within wheels within wheels, and it should have come as no surprise to me that the testimonial dinner, while ostensibly for Lynch, was in reality a public sounding board for the man that Hague wanted to take Lynch's place. In his prime, Herr Doktor Goebbels could have taken propaganda lessons from Hague. When I walked into the dining room the night of the dinner, one of the mayor's chief lieutenants was in charge, briefing the reporters on the kind of story he wanted to see in tomorrow's newspapers. He had a band seated at the rear, and a bar and bartender to see that everyone was made suitably mellow.

However, even Hague didn't win all the time. The man he wanted for the job had been suspended by the State Price and Rationing Board for irregularities as chairman of a particular panel, and when he came up for appointment in Jersey City he was turned down. Instead, Louis Carr, a school principal and Lynch's choice, got the job. The whole thing was, for me, an object lesson in the deceitfulness of politics and in how easily men will sell their honor to win an approving nod from the boss.

In 1942, as I told you, we lost some of our finest boys. But also, in 1942—November 15, to be exact—we celebrated the diamond jubilee of St. Michael's; and what a glorious day it

207

was. Believe it or not, we started to prepare for it three years before. At that time, I asked Dr. Julia Harney, our long-time organist, to prepare a short history of the parish in booklet form. She, you may recall, enjoyed the unique distinction of having served in the administrations of all five pastors. At first I hesitated to ask her because she was then assistant superintendent of schools in Jersey City, and I knew that her tasks were enormous.

She not only accepted, but seemed to derive much pleasure from the work. When the booklet appeared, on the great day, it turned out to be perfection itself and was one of the big features of the celebration.

I wrote a short foreword to it, and in it I said: "Since the parish began, in 1867, there have been only five pastors, and the history of their lives is the history of St. Michael's.

"The first two were among the great churchmen of their times, while the fourth possessed talents and merits of so high an order that he was raised to the dignity of the episcopacy. The third pastor was called to his reward after only three years, but in that brief span of time he effected a major renovation of the church. The fifth and present pastor, and writer of this foreword, knows his limitations too well to place himself in the category of his predecessors and leaves to a kindly posterity the judgment to be placed on his unworthiness. . . ."

On that day, I sang the Solemn votive Mass of Thanksgiving of St. Michael the Archangel, assisted by Father Edward Casserly, S.S.J., as deacon, Father Mark Kennedy, O.F.M., as subdeacon, Right Reverend Monsignor John C. McClary, vicar-general, as archpriest, and Father Henry Mackin as master of ceremonies. His Excellency, the Most Reverend Thomas Joseph Walsh, Archbishop of Newark, presided, and His Excellency, the Most Reverend William A. Griffin,

Bishop of Trenton, preached the sermon. Many other high-ranking dignitaries of church and city and state were there, and a multitude of priests came from far and near. Our own dearly beloved people of St. Michael's filled the balance of the vaulted nave, and it was a colorful sight as the stately ceremonies of the Mass proceeded and clouds of incense lifted through the double-colonetted attic of the baldachino.

I would be less than human if I didn't confess that I treasure the words of Bishop Griffin. He traced the history of St. Michael's, and he told of the accomplishment of the pastors, and when he came to me he said:

"Nor need I prolong this discourse by recounting the zealous labors of your present beloved pastor, whose relation to you and to all his predecessors has been unique. For, since his ordination to the holy priesthood he has served here continuously as curate and pastor for twenty-four years; he has seen the longest service in this one parish after Monsignors de Concilio and Sheppard; he has been curate under his three immediate predecessors and thus has forged a strong and valuable and effective link between their administrations. To my certain knowledge, he is the only priest in the diocese who has been full time principal of a Catholic high school. With his fine personality, his great mental endowments, his power of organization and his scrupulous attention to detail, he grew with the high school and left the impress of his genial character upon all its graduates. Now, as pastor, he enjoys a wider field for the flowering of all his fine manly and priestly qualities among a people to whom he has given generously of himself and between whom and himself there is a strong bond of affection.

"He has always held in reverence, and zealously guarded, the best traditions of this grand old parish (and it has many traditions) and his accomplishments in the field of education and charity, especially as spiritual director of the St. Vincent de Paul Society and as Vice-moderator of the Mount Carmel Guild, are known to all in the parish and throughout the city."

Afterward dinner was served to the hierarchy and the priests in the auditorium, and to all nuns in the convent. A great day had come and gone, but it was, in my mind, fitting that St. Michael's should pause in its march through time to celebrate its seventy-fifth birthday. The remainder of the week was given over to celebrating, and on Monday a High Mass was sung for all deceased priests, nuns, and people of the parish. This Mass was offered by Monsignor Mark S. Duffy, pastor of St. Aloysius' Church, Jersey City, and a former curate at St. Michael's. On Tuesday a Low Mass was celebrated for all the living priests, sisters, and people of St. Michael's by Father Tom Curry, pastor of St. Bridget's Church, and a former boy of the parish; on Wednesday, another boy of St. Michael's, the late Monsignor John J. Murphy, pastor of Sacred Heart Church in Vailsburg, celebrated a Low Mass for all St. Michael's boys then in service; on Thursday, still another St. Michael's boy, Father Joe Dooling, now pastor of St. Francis Xavier Church in Newark, sang a High Mass for the children of St. Michael's School.

The ceremonies were solemn and sacred, but my mind kept going back to that day, Sunday, September 29, 1872, when Archbishop Bayley of Baltimore laid the cornerstone of the church. I had a yellowed old copy of the *Evening Journal* of the following day, and this is what it says:

"The procession preceding the exercises at the Church was a very long one. In the line of march were 6,000 members of the Ancient Order of Hibernians, also about 6,000 members of the St. Patrick's Mutual Alliance Benevolent Association, besides a large representation of the Mutual Democratic Alliance and St. Peter's, St. Patricks, St. Michael's, St. Bridget's Shamrock Working Men's and numerous other temperance and benevolent organizations. Passaic, Paterson and Newark, as well as New York and Brooklyn were well represented. The ancient Gallow Glasses attracted much attention in their peculiar uniforms, long beards, helmets, broad axes, etc. Frank McDonald acted as Grand Marshal. He rode a magnificent horse and was decorated with an immense green sash and chapeau. He was the admiration of all the good-looking Irish girls along the route. The procession, at three o'clock, went down to the ferry, where it met the New York and Brooklyn brethren; then the procession turned around and, with six bands of music playing and any number of Irish and American banners fluttering, marched up to Hamilton Square where, at the southern entrance, stood Fathers Concilio and Cannon waiting to receive them."

The account goes on to tell how the priests took up a collection with wooden buckets as the people passed through the gates and of how the reverend fathers filled six buckets with money, ranging from five-dollar bills down to small-denomination stamps. The Archbishop laid the cornerstone with ceremony, following which he mounted the platform and delivered a short address. Rain was impending and his remarks were brief—briefer than he had intended.

"I had better go on speaking now," he said, "as it may take all day for the crowd to get in. You have witnessed this afternoon the dedication of the church we are in to St. Michael the Archangel. I need not tell you that this was a great work in that you built a house not for man but for God. Were you to erect these walls of gold, you could not express too much your love to the Almighty and the Saviour Who is your guide to eternal life. The great objects for which churches are built are first, the celebration of the Holy Sacrifice which, according to Divine Scripture, shall be offered up in the House of God day and night. Here also the sacraments are to be administered, and here will be preached to you the true word of God.

"I intended making a discourse on this matter today. I wanted to talk to you on God's truths as interpreted in His truthfulness and integrity. But the weather is so uncertain that I will not enter upon this discussion. It involves an argument and if it should begin to rain my argument would be cut short just at the time I might be getting warmed to my subject.

"I will address you only on church building. In building this structure you have acted in accordance with the Catholic Church, which has always been a church builder. She began work in this way sixteen hundred and more years ago in the catacombs of Rome, when the early Christians were persecuted. It has been argued that, at that time, the services of the Church were conducted with Quaker-like simplicity. These declarations have no foundations in history or fact. None who have visited the catacombs but will see that the early Christians were not content with mere bare walls for the celebration of the Holy Sacrifice.

"Even in those days of early persecution, they began the erection of those beautiful arches, thus showing a taste for the beautiful in religion, which afterwards, in better times, culminated in the erection of those grand old Gothic cathedrals of Europe which stand for all time as poems wrought in stone. Lucian, who by the way was an old scoffer and the Voltaire of his day, has written in his poems hatred of Christianity and he dwells upon the inconsistency of the Christians, who, while pretending to be poor, used such huge sums of money on their churches.

"Some have said that these churches were built by bad kings with money they had stolen. It won't do, however, for the rich people today to make this charge, for there is as much stealing now as then. The only difference is the men in medieval times made restitution for their sins and did penance by building churches, but now they don't. . . ."

At this point, a drenching rain came down, and the archbishop closed with the remark that he did not see any way in which he could stop the shower and so he would say no more. It took the tremendous crowd a long while to get away from the church grounds.

These are the things that crossed my mind, seventy-five years later.

It is an ironic truth that at family reunions no voice ever warns you that this is the last one. And so it happened with me. In the summer of 1942, my younger brother, James, my older brother, Father Raymond, and I rented a cottage for one month at Awosting, on Greenwood Lake, to be with our mother. These were the carefree hours. These were the hours full of love and great joy. With the exception of Father—may God be merciful to him, always—the family was together again.

In spirit we were kids again, and mother wasn't seventy-five; she was young and bustling and pretty, and time fled backward thirty years or so, and we sat in the evenings remembering and remembering and remembering. We swam and fished and dozed in the sun, and we cooked for Mother and took turns washing and drying the dishes. It was thirty days of grace—thirty memorable days. But no warning voice said, "This is the last time. . . ."

In November, Dr. Dwyer of Paterson sent for me. He said that he had been in fairly constant attendance on Mother and that serious abdominal symptoms had become manifest and it was his suggestion that I consult another doctor. I conferred with Dr. Frank McLoughlin, medical director of St. Francis Hospital, across the street from the church. He listened to all the testimony, and he looked at me and said that if it was his mother he would send her to the Leahy Clinic in Boston. There, he told me, I would find a Dr. Cattell, one of the three best abdominal surgeons in the United States.

On December 7 I accompanied my mother to Boston. She turned to me and smiled and said she guessed that maybe this was her personal Pearl Harbor. I told her that it was nothing of the kind and that in no time at all she'd be well again and good for a number of years. I was wrong, but if the occasion arose again I'd say the same thing.

The examination was made, and the diagnosis indicated immediate surgery. Mother and I stood and prepared to leave to think it over when Dr. Leahy himself, in a peremptory voice, demanded to know what we had come there for anyway. Mother turned back and said that she had decided to stay.

Dr. Cattell performed two operations, and after the first one Mother suffered the tortures of the damned. It was necessary to sear off some skin around the incision by electricity, and Mother said that it was almost more than a human being could stand. Father Raymond, James, and I took turns shuttling back and forth to Boston, so that one of us would always be on hand to comfort her. In January, 1943, she came home. She had been given the best of care by doctors and nurses, and one of the nurses returned with her to stay awhile in Paterson.

The Leahy Clinic had done its part and more, but Mother enjoyed little respite from pain after that. In the middle of June we decided that it would be better if she checked into St.

Francis Hospital in Jersey City, where she would get the finest attention. Dr. McLoughlin took care of Mother himself. It was a very hot summer, and she had her good days and her bad days. When I asked Dr. McLoughlin about her chances, he would only shrug and tell me that it might be a long time and it might be a short time; he didn't know.

Mother was tiny and brave. There wasn't a whimper of complaint from her, even though, sometimes, a spasm of agony would erase her smile for a moment. But only for a moment. She had had the last rites of the Church, and she received Holy Communion as often as her condition would allow. She worried more about me than about herself, and she said that I looked tired, and wouldn't I please go away and rest for a few days. Every fiber of my being told me that this was wrong, but she kept to the subject and held my hand in hers and kept asking me to please go somewhere and relax; that she'd be all right until I got back. So I went away, reluctantly, and kept myself on constant call, knowing that James would be there every day. When the call came, I hurried back to the hospital, and it is my eternal regret that I missed saying good-by by a few minutes. That was Friday night, July 30, 1943. Mother was seventy-six. As I stroked her hair, she seemed to be in a dreamless sleep; a rest well earned.

She was a loving and faithful wife and mother—the best there is. All her life she had given of herself to others—to Father, to Raymond, to James, to me, to her neighbors, her friends. For more than thirty-five years she had been engaged in charitable work, especially the Mount Carmel Guild. Now she had no more to give, and she had nothing left for herself.

Tributes came from all over. These are the tender, inadequate words which cannot console the heart but keep the body from shaking with sobs. Bishop McLaughlin of Pater-

215

son paid a personal visit to the house. A message of sympathy came from Bishop Boland. A delegation of three hundred persons from St. Michael's Parish traveled to Paterson for the wake. There were representatives from Mount Carmel Guild, the Altar Society of St. Joseph's Church in Paterson, St. Joseph's Hospital, the Paterson Women's Club, the Red Cross, the Jesuit Mothers' Aid Society, the Bayley Seton League—so, so many. Bishop Griffin of Trenton presided at the Solemn Requiem Mass in St. Joseph's Church, Paterson, sung by her first son, Father Raymond, while I assisted as deacon. Many priests filled the sanctuary, and nuns from many orders of the Church knelt in the pews near Mother's casket. My youngest brother James led the procession of hundreds of mourners from all walks of life, including Senator Harry Williams, the Honorable Harry B. Haines, and Mother's faithful servant, Lily Cleary. It was a touching farewell for a valiant lady.

What did I think about in those final hours? When I had time to meditate, when I wasn't receiving condolences, I thought of the days of long ago when the three of us were at her knees. I thought of gaslights in the streets and oil lamps on the table. I thought of big, gruff-looking men with muttonchop whiskers and of high-buttoned shoes. Women, in those days, wore black or white cotton stockings. There were no others. The female form was covered to the instep. At the beach men wore two-piece bathing suits, and women donned caps, blouses, skirts, stockings, and shoes before they entered the water. It was a Victorian era of strict morals, and children were seen but not heard. No women, except the kind the men whispered about, ever smoked or drank.

The horse and buggy were standard equipment, and a man with a matched pair of spanking bays was automatically rich. For minutes John Bunny laughed in a short, silent flicker, and the audience laughed with him although they could not hear him. The two-step and the waltz were popular. So were the gallop, the polka, and the schottische. Loin of pork was eleven cents a pound, and the butcher threw in a pound of calves' liver for nothing. Five cents would keep a boy in candy for the better part of a week, and a man who made twenty dollars a week was a responsible citizen and a good provider.

As I was thinking, I could see the changes that my mother had lived through. For the first time I could see how her world, so compact and neat when she was a bride, had broadened and degenerated as she grew older. In 1911, when I was entering college, the age of innocence seemed to be dying. Skirts began to get shorter, and the dresses became flimsier. The mystery of feminine charm began to dissipate. One early movie magnate said, "Two and two make four, four and four make eight, and sex and sex make millions."

Chaperons became passé, and matters which had hitherto been accepted as dogma were now questioned. The permanency of marriage became the butt of cruel vaudeville jokes, and family prayer was considered old-fashioned. Those who could write carried the banners of this moral revolution, and in the vanguard were Sigmund Freud, the Persian skeptic of the "Rubáiyát," George Bernard Shaw, and H. G. Wells, with their revolutionary and devastating ideas, plays, and novels. They and others broke down the taboos, and they proclaimed a new freedom, which, in fact, was just an old license.

Penance was scorned; sin was king. The eternal life was swapped outright for the gay life. The old values of decency were worthless, and man, in his madness, plunged into a war in which, at one point, field-artillery pieces were jammed hubcap to hubcap for 16 miles, spitting death. When it was

217

over, the accent was on youth—Flaming Youth. At twenty-four, a young man named F. Scott Fitzgerald pointed the way to sexual independence with a novel called *This Side of Paradise*. Young men who had carried guns in the war continued to carry them when they came home. We had the era of the one-way ride. A girl who couldn't swig gin and lie on a couch with a stranger was a wet blanket, and was invited out but once.

It was neopaganism, but it wasn't new to the Church. Down through the centuries, she had seen these mad movements come and go, come and go, and come and go again. She is not behind the times. She has seen times without number. The times revolve around her. When her children get back to her, they are in the light. When they swing away from her, they are in darkness. The Church knows that the tissue of the mind and the heart remains unchanged from age to age. Education may become more widespread, and knowledge more extensive. But when it is pagan, it remains what it always has been—a way of life without God.

The second chapter of the Book of Wisdom has a vivid account of what went on in those days. In reading it one is struck with the similarity of the things that have happened in our own century. St. Augustine's description, in Book II of his *City of God*, of the goings on in the Roman Empire 1500 years ago could well be used as a portrait of the last fifty years. And Augustine's opinion is most valuable not only because he was an intellectual giant, but because he lived in an age when paganism and Christianity were locked in a death struggle. He himself had a checkered sex career and finally embraced Catholicism. He could speak as one who knew. He had seen and passed through all the vagaries paganism had to offer.

Moral values and criteria are of God, and they can never

218

change. The American bishops recently stated what the Church has held since the beginning:

"Morality viewed in its entirety has three dimensions: height, depth, and breadth. In its height it soars up to God, the Supreme Being from Whom it takes the definitive measure of what is true and good. In its depth it penetrates the heart of man, laying hold of his entire personality so that even his innermost thoughts and motives are subject to its rule. In its breadth it embraces man in every station and condition of life and establishes mutual rights and duties. . . . God's will therefore is the measure of man. It is the standard by which all human actions must meet the test of their rightness or wrongness. What conforms to God's will is right and what goes counter to His will is wrong."

My thoughts showed me that the world my mother knew was no longer here. She had outlived it, just as she had outlived my father and their friends. She had lived to see them go, one by one, each a distinct wrench to the troubled heart, and now, when the world was alien to her code and her faith, she had passed away.

I was comforted.

11

In december of the same year, I was twenty-five years a priest—all of them spent in St. Michael's. My intention was to offer a Mass of Thanksgiving quietly, on this day, and let it go at that. Some close friends pointed out, however, that the people of a parish welcome an occasion like this to show their love and reverence for the priesthood, and these friends reminded me that a priest doesn't have to wait until he expires to hear kind words, that God entrusted His ministry to men, not angels, and that no one could be more human than a priest. They argued that the people would not be doing honor to me but to the priesthood.

It sounded reasonable. The priest who meditates every day knows his own limitations and will attribute any graces he possesses, not to himself but to the great God Who gave them to him. He will listen, smiling, to the nice things that are said about him and he will apply to them "the usual clerical discount."

In the parlance of the times, my "arm was twisted," and I agreed to a Solemn Mass of Thanksgiving. Dr. Julia Harney presided at the organ and directed her fine choir. His Excellency, the Most Reverend Thomas Joseph Walsh, Archbishop of Newark, graced the occasion by his presence. Bishop Griffin, who was to have preached the sermon, became ill at the last moment, and I phoned Father Raymond Kennedy, a Jesuit whom I knew very well, and I asked him if he would pinch-hit. He agreed. Although he had precious little time to prepare anything, Father Kennedy delivered a beautiful discourse. The vicar-general, monsignori, priests, a large number of sisters, friends, and people of the parish were present.

After the Mass, I responded briefly.

"In the preface of the Mass today we said: *Gratias agamus Domino Deo Nostro*—let us give thanks to the Lord our God. And so, with a grateful heart on this occasion, we thank the Creator Who made us, ordained us, and spared us for twenty-five years in the sacred ministry. Every good and perfect gift is from above and cometh down from the Father of Light. We attribute all that we are or have become to the love and bounty of our Father, God. 'What is there that you have not received and if you have received why do you glory as if you had not received?'

"We pay tribute this day to our beloved parents, both gone to God. We owe them ever so much, and would that they could be here to rejoice with us today. We regret especially that our mother, deceased but a short time, was not spared to participate in this occasion. They both received from us a special remembrance in the Mass of today.

"And, most Reverend Archbishop, it is no ordinary honor that you have paid us by your coming here this morning. It was more than gracious that so great a prelate could find time

221

to adorn with his presence the silver anniversary of one of the least of his diocesan priests. For the courtesy and kindness you have shown us today, as well as for the many favors and considerations of the past, we are deeply grateful.

"We thank Monsignor McClary, our vicar-general, Monsignor Hughes, our chancellor, Monsignors Costelloe and Clark, Father Dooling, our assistant ministers, all the monsignori and priests both secular and religious, the reverend sisters, visiting relatives, friends, and parishioners.

"May peace and joy come to you this day. God's blessing on you, every one."

Dinner was then served to the archbishop, the monsignori, and the priests in the rectory. Another dinner was served to sisters, close friends, and relatives in the convent. The next evening a testimonial dinner was tendered by parishioners at the Plaza Hotel in Jersey City. On Tuesday morning a reception was held by the students of the high school, and on Tuesday evening a reception by parishioners in the auditorium. Wednesday evening concluded the festivities with a reception given by the nurses in St. Francis Hospital.

According to all the natural laws I had passed the two-thirds mark in my priestly life.

Of course, throughout all this, the current of parish life went on as usual. The doorbell of the rectory rang all day long and again in the evening from seven o'clock until nine. People came in with problems, salesmen with their Mixmasters and their vacuum cleaners and books. Meetings of various societies were held in the auditorium, and plans were made for Communion breakfasts; fund-raising campaigns were laid out, and cultural programs were blueprinted. The auditorium was like a hive full of bees for six days of each week. In fact, some nights there would be as many as three meetings going on in various parts of the auditorium at the same time.

The high light of each year, for me, was always First Holy Communion Sunday. This was the morning when the little ones received the body and blood of Christ for the first time. The boys wore blue suits, or white, and the girls wore white lacy dresses and veils. It was a big day, a great day, in fact, because we made it bigger than just a First Communion Sunday.

For months the children were prepared by the sisters. They studied their catechisms until they knew the answers backward. When the sisters were finished with them, the youngsters, at the tender age of seven, knew the difference between right and wrong, the difference between grace and sin, the laws of God and of Holy Mother Church.

But what made it a bigger day was that we inaugurated a policy of having the mothers and fathers go to the altar rail with the child, and receive Communion with their offspring. You can't have any idea what a touching and wonderful sight that is, unless you've seen it.

About a week before the day, I sent out letters to all the parents.

DEAR PARENTS:

On Laetare Sunday, your child will receive First Holy Communion. What memories this must bring back to you! It was the great day of your life.

It's going to be just the same with your child and I know that you will be there. In addition, however, I want you to receive Communion with your child—daddy on the right hand side and mamma on the left. How edifying that will be and what an impression that will make.

As your child sees you receive he will realize that Communion is not just for a day, but something that should be continued throughout life.

Looking forward expectantly to seeing you at the altar on that day, I am

Yours sincerely,

FATHER MCWILLIAMS

When the letter was mailed, we told the child about it, and for a solid week the parents were bombarded with reminders to get to confession so that all three could receive Communion together on the following Sunday. The way it worked out it was better than a mission! I've seen faces at the altar rail on that Sunday that hadn't been inside a church for years. I've seen estranged parents standing on either side of a little girl, looking sheepishly at each other, each hoping that the other would make the first move toward a reconciliation. I've seen others who lived together, but who were not on speaking terms, submerge their differences in the wonder of the innocent heart they were laying at the feet of God. Then, too, there is the memory that the child will always carry with him—that on the day of his First Communion his mother and his father received with him.

Altogether, we had lost about 500 families from the parish, so confirmation was not held more often than every three years. This, too, was a big moment, but the confirmees had to be in their twelfth year, and it didn't move me the way the seven-year-olds could, and did.

I was most impressed, after the war, to learn that in the battle for Guadalcanal the United States Marines captured the ruins of a missionary Catholic church. Their chaplain promised that, as most of the pews were still standing and the altar was intact, he would say Mass there the following Sunday. Meanwhile, the natives had been hiding in the hills, but when they saw the preparations going on in the church, the word was passed and they came down silently and filed into the church in time for Mass.

The Catholic marines stood on one side of the church; the ignorant natives on the other. When the priest began his Mass, he was astonished to find that the natives made all the responses in Latin! The marines didn't know the responses. Some wonderful missionary with patience had taught these poor people the proper way to participate in the Holy Sacrifice of the Mass.

It irritated me to think that here in America we are so smug about our Catholicity. We know all the answers, but from Sunday to Sunday all we do is kneel and stand and sit. We are mute. So, for twelve months we priests of St. Michael's talked about the Mass and its parts, and its meanings, and its symbolism. We also distributed, free, a copy of the leaflet missal, so that the people would understand the Mass and be able to follow it step by step. Then we put regular missals on sale containing all the Masses for Sundays and holydays of obligation.

The response was fair. It could have been better. I found that it isn't easy to change a habit pattern. But that didn't stop me. I'm still trying, and I can report progress. More and more parishioners are using the missals; thus they are learning more and more about the Mass.

From time to time we also tried to get the people to attend Mass every morning. The League of Daily Mass is an example of what I mean, and it was one of the great experiences of my life to see how fruitful our efforts were. You see, the Mass is the great act in a priest's life. He begins his day with that august function. *That* he must celebrate fruitfully and well. Failure to do so would render all else of little value. He may have brilliant attainments of mind and of heart; he may have an attractive personality and be much sought after by his parishioners, but it is the Mass that matters, and he can be a great priest only if he prepares for it properly and makes it the most important thing of his life. And it naturally follows that his deep realization of the value of the Mass must inspire him to seek greater participation on the part of the laity in this most indispensable function.

There is nothing more sacred in the eyes of the God who made us than the Christian home. It is the bedrock on which a healthy society depends. Christ thought so much of it that He caused Himself to be born in the bosom of a human family and lived in it exclusively for most of His life. His first miracle was in behalf of a newly formed family at Cana. He changed water into wine to relieve their embarrassment.

He might have come into this world surrounded with a bodyguard of angels. He might have appeared full grown with great panoply and power and asserted Himself as complete Lord and Master. But then the decay of society would have remained unchecked. Its evils would have continued as before. Christ wanted to start from the bottom up, and so He began with the family.

Imitating her Master, the Church has always stood for the sanctity of the family, the sacredness of the home. The ills that afflict them today are the same as they were 1900 years ago. Faithful to her trust, the Church must defend these institutions.

In my parish the spirit of the family is never better exemplified than on graduation night. That is when you see the shining faces across the footlights; the proudness when Daddy grasps Mamma's hands, and their glance at each other reads, "Well, we've done a good job!" That's when you can almost see them retraverse the years down to their wedding, and they think of all the fun and the hardships, the laughter and the tears, the quarrels and the kiss of forgiveness, the trouble and the miracle of birth, the skinned knees and the bad report cards, the hits and the errors—that's when they see family life in its entirety. If ever, that's when they see that each person is never so important as the whole family. The family good, the family welfare, takes priority over the wishes and the desires of any member of it.

On that night I too see the heart of the family more clearly than at any other time. Whether the students are graduated, as President Taft once said, "Cum laude, summa cum laude, or mirabile dictu," they are graduated, and the ecstasy of the family can be no greater than the feeling of satisfaction in the breasts of the priests and the sisters, who have given their best to make good Americans and good Catholics. If any sight is happier than high-school graduation night, it is kindergarten graduation. When the tiny ones come on-stage in their caps and gowns, they are terrific, and the capacity-filled hall of young mothers and fathers—each with eyes for only one tot—is something to behold.

Take away the family, and man goes back to the cave.

Those war years represented busy days and nights for me. To keep all my appointments I needed a fire engine at least. In addition to my priestly duties, which were multitudinous, I was a member of the Ration Board, Community Chest, Citizens' Advisory Committee, American Red Cross, American Cancer Society, Public Health Nursing Committee, the Council of Social Agencies, and St. Francis Hospital Training School Board.

In none of these cases did I seek the job, and in none did I shirk it when it was offered. I would not lend my name to be used solely on a letterhead. If they wanted me, they also wanted my best efforts and my best opinions. Each of these agencies made a contribution to life and public welfare in Jersey City, and, as I told you before, I believe that if a priest can spare the time, he should help the general public and he should be seen among non-Catholics. I remember reading that St. Francis Xavier, to win the hearts of others when he was on the high seas, once sat down at table and played cards with the deck hands.

I was about as busy as I could be without risking a nervous breakdown, and yet more sorrow was headed my way. My brother, Father Raymond, died on the morning of February 12, 1946, at the age of fifty-three. He died in St. Francis Hospital, and, in a way, it affected me more than the deaths of my mother and my father. Scholastically, we had practically grown up together. He was in my sophomore class at Seton Hall College. Ray's great speciality was science, and in 1919 he was placed in charge of the biology department at Holy Cross College. In 1922 he returned to Woodstock, Maryland, to complete his theological studies, and he was ordained on June 14, 1926.

Whereas my interests were parochial and civic, his were scholastic. He applied himself to his studies and his research so diligently that he brought on a nervous breakdown while in his tertianship at St. Andrew's in Poughkeepsie. The master of novices, Father John O'Rourke, S.J., advised Father Raymond to withdraw from the Society of Jesus and to seek incardination in his native diocese of Newark. At the time, Bishop O'Connor having died, Monsignor John A. Duffy, the vicar-general, was acting as administrator pending the appointment of a new bishop. Monsignor Duffy, who had been one of Ray's instructors at Seton Hall, welcomed him and received him pro tempore. He had no power to incardinate Father Raymond.

I felt miserable. Ray was older; he had gone through a more difficult course of study than I, and now his nervous system had failed and he moved about almost aimlessly. No one who has not undergone the throes of a nervous breakdown can understand the mental torture, the agony, the despondency, the feeling of hell on earth. When he convalesced, it left such a permanent mark on him that he could never get a permanent status anywhere. After I had been pastor of St. Michael's for a year, with the kindness and permission of the Archbishop, Father Raymond came to live with me.

I assigned him to teach biology in the high school, and he conducted the course with great skill, as I knew he would. Some effects of his illness still remained, however, and, in addition, he worried too much and contracted ulcers. A little later on he sustained a coronary occlusion and was rushed across the street to St. Francis. He recovered. Three years later he suffered another attack. When I enquired about his condition, the doctor told me that he would be out in two weeks. I relaxed.

I had a large meeting of Catholic War Veterans one night, and, in the middle of the session, the doctor phoned and told me that Father Raymond would die that night or the next morning. I excused myself and hurried across the street. My dear brother was indeed dying. The pain he was suffering was almost unendurable, and he was taking large doses of morphine. Still, in his agony, he knew that something serious was afoot when he looked up from his bed and saw me standing there with Dr. Garibaldi and Dr. McLoughlin.

He was dying, and there was nothing I could do about it.

He had borne his cross for years, in silence, and now I felt helpless, futile, just standing there and looking. I went to the next room and awakened old Father Peter, a Franciscan, and I asked him to prepare Father Raymond for death. I administered Extreme Unction, gave the last blessing, and recited the prayers for the dying. Emotionally it tore me apart. When I came to that prayer, "Depart, O Christian soul, out of this sinful world, in the name of God, the Father Almighty, Who created thee; in the name of Jesus Christ, the Son of the Living God, Who suffered and died for thee . . ." I choked up and couldn't proceed. I had to wait a few minutes to regain my composure. I told you that it makes a difference when the life that is ebbing away is so close and so dear to you, and this time it got me and it got me bad. He was still alive, still breathing like a deep sleeper who snores, when the prayers were finished. It was now two o'clock in the morning, and I went back to the rectory to get some rest.

At dawn I was back at the bedside, and Father Raymond was still alive. But it was clear now, from the increased labor of breathing, that the end was not far off. The sister superior from the convent, Sister Grace Miriam, was there, and so was the Franciscan sister of that floor. They were on their knees, reciting the Holy Rosary, and, in silence, I knelt and joined them. When we were finished, I asked Father Raymond if there was anything further we could do for him. He turned his eyes to me, eyes swimming with remembrance, and he murmured faintly that he would like to see Father Viccaro of the neighboring Holy Rosary Church. I was in the midst of phoning when Sister Grace Miriam came to me and told me that my brother had died.

We buried him from St. Michael's Church. It was the last honor I could accord a brother whom I loved deeply. One hundred and forty-nine Masses were arranged for him, and he was entered in eleven purgatorial associations. Bishop Griffin gave the Absolution, and there must have been sixty priests and monsignori in attendance at the Mass.

He was interred in the family plot in Holy Sepulchre Cemetery in Paterson. He had come home, at last.

On the lighter side, at the age of fifty-four I decided to buy a small sailboat. It was a silly whim, but I had seen people up at Highland Lakes swinging along, like great white swans and with such grace and ease that I decided to try it too. In the spring of 1948, then, I bought a "Wood Pussy" from the Palmer Scott Boat Company, of Bedford, Massachusetts. It was 13½ feet long, and about 5½ feet on the beam. It would hold four people comfortably, and when it arrived I was as eager as a kid on the night before Christmas. Outside, the temperature was about forty degrees, and a stiff wind was blowing down from the hills, but I couldn't wait.

With me were John Tiedemann and Billy Connors. I invited them to join me in a "christening" of my brand-new boat. Happily, they knew just as much about sailing as I, which was nothing. No instruction book had come with the craft, but what did that matter? You just hoisted the sail and sailed it. Nothing to it. At least that's what I thought.

Well, we hoisted the snowy-white sail, and we took off, flying down the lake. It was wonderful. This indeed was the life. We hoped that some of the early vacationers were watching, because we were somebody. We got down the lake a way, and I decided to turn her around and take her back. I swung the tiller, and the next thing I knew we were all in the freezing water and the boat was upside down.

We were all fully dressed. I even had my glasses on. Neither John nor Billy could swim, and they clung to the top of the overturned hull for dear life. I was the only one who could swim, and I was wearing a Windbreaker, so there was no danger of my breaking world's swimming records getting to shore. But I made it, promising I'd be right back with help. Fortunately, on shore stood Paul Barta, the Highland Lakes policeman, and he sure got an eye opener when he saw who the landlubber was. He drove me back to the cabin, and I changed into dry clothes and drove back for the boys. By the time I got there, they had the boat back into shore, right side up, and they were chattering with cold. I drove them back and gave them dry clothes, and we congratulated ourselves on being real salty sailors.

Later, we bailed the boat out and paddled it back to the little dock. By now I was hoping that none of the early vacationers saw how elegant we were, skimming over the waves. After I acquired some experience sailing the boat, I tried to rationalize my mistake of that first day, and the only way I can account for it is that I must have jibed the boat, instead of coming about.

Later in that summer I was standing on the little dock, and John was sitting in the *Wood Pussy* with the sail up. A steady breeze was blowing, and somehow John lost control of the boat. I saw the boom coming my way with increasing speed, and I knew that it would send me flying; so, discretion being better than valor, I dove overboard with all my clothes on. When I came up, sputtering, the laughter of my lake neighbors rang in my ears.

But the pay-off came one day when I tried to feed the rope back through an eyelet at the top of the mast. The mast is 20 feet high, and I unwisely rigged up a ladder, standing it on the bows and leaning it against the top of the mast. You'd have to have the poise of a tightrope walker to balance yourself against that stick of a mast. The Hennessy Brothers Incorporated—Father Francis A. of St. Aedan's, Jersey City, and Father Edward D. of Holy Trinity, Hackensack, New Jersey—were staying with their family a few cottages away from mine. They saw my distress, and they came down to help me.

Father Frank mounted the ladder while the rest of us stood in the cockpit of the boat watching him. He got to the top all right, and he was just feeding the rope into the eyelet when he swayed and—kerplunk!—into the lake he went. This so upset the balance of the boat that Father Ed and I were tossed out of the cockpit into the water.

We did then what we should have done in the first place: beached the boat, turned it on its side, and threaded the eyelet. Just how stupid can you get? Come to think of it, I furnished so many boating surprises to my neighbors, the Sholzes, that they must have felt kind of lonesome when I went home.

12

IN JERSEY CITY there was a recurrent political joke. It went
like this:

TEACHER: Who made the Jersey City Fire Department?
PUPIL: Mayor Hague.
TEACHER: Who made the Jersey City Police Department?
PUPIL: Mayor Hague.
TEACHER: Who made the world?
PUPIL: God made the world.
CHORUS OF PUPILS: You dirty Republican!

The thought behind the joke isn't as much exaggerated as
you might think. For over thirty years Frank Hague was
almost a demigod to the people of Jersey City and Hudson
County, and only slightly smaller in rank to the Democratic
party of the state of New Jersey and the nation. *The New
Yorker* once published a cartoon showing Mussolini, Hitler,
and Hague joining hands across a table. Underneath, it read,
"The signing of the Berlin–Rome–Jersey City Axis."

Hague was a bigger phenomenon of his times, and more ruthless, than Boss Crump of Memphis or Boss Pendergast of Missouri. The only fights he ever lost were those he secretly chose to lose, and then only because he had sewed up the opposition so that, in effect, they too were working for him. I've already told you that politics is the daily bread of every man, woman, and literate child in Jersey City. It is what baseball is to Brooklyn, what football is to South Bend, what stocks are to Wall Street, what the motion-picture industry is to Hollywood, what a spot of tea is to an Englishman. Nothing can happen in Jersey City that is not attributable, in some way, to politics.

Hague, as mayor, came up for election every four years. If 140,000 votes were cast, it was nothing for him to win by 85,000 or more. In these campaigns Hague would take the stump, his right index finger pointing at the crowds, warning them of the dire things that would happen to them if his group was not returned to power. The harder he hit the fragile Republican opposition, the more they seemed to like it. At these rallies, it was not unusual to see 125,000 persons, out of a total population of 316,000, standing for hours waiting to hear the master speak. Before he spoke, a man named Napolitano would set off thousands of dollars' worth of fireworks, and huge exploding rockets would boom into the sky to shatter the ears, followed by graceful aerial umbrellas of red and green and blue.

The people were hypnotized. It was said, by Hague's enemies, that he didn't have to campaign. All he had to do was to put his name on the ballot and rest in his beautiful home in Florida, and the people would claw each other to be the first to vote for him.

A good psychologist might tell you that the answer to the Hague riddle is that he represented the father image to the

people; that is, they looked up to him as one would to an old-fashioned father, a person who is benevolent and vengeful, just and harsh—one who knows better than you what is good for you. He did many fine things, too. He built one of the finest medical centers in the world, and named the maternity hospital after his mother, Margaret Hague. He took a shift-less, graft-ridden police department and made it a model of efficiency, and drove the drinkers out of uniform. He bought the finest equipment for the fire department and reduced the underwriters' premiums against property. The poor people (who voted right) were given jobs and free operations in the hospital. Add to this the fact that he had the most prodigious memory of the twentieth century—a memory that enabled him to remember almost everything about everybody—and that he could dispense favors at his whim, and you have a fair idea of what a complex character he was.

Well, in 1947 Frank Hague announced that he was retiring. Politics, he said, had been good to him, and now he was quitting. If the word had been passed around that the world was coming to an end at sundown, the people could not have been more stunned. Hague was over seventy, but he was vigorous, and his spine was as straight as a West Pointer's. Somehow, to the 300,000 inhabitants of the city, the announcement didn't seem "kosher." It didn't fit into any of the facts of political life as they knew it.

Still, things began to happen fast once Hague had called the play, and, as these events occurred, the people sat back and said, "Ahhh, now I see what he means." Almost overnight Joseph Colford stepped down as a city commissioner and became a county freeholder. Philip McGovern, city clerk, resigned his job and became commissioner of public works; John Prout, a clerk and a ward leader, catapulted to the top and became commissioner of parks and public improvements.

And then came the pay-off. The city commissioners, without a smile on their faces, solemnly elected Frank Hague's favorite nephew, Frank Hague Eggers, as the new mayor.

Hague was starting a family dynasty. Eggers, a rotund man who had personality and ability, might have made a fine mayor, but he was hamstrung because he was his uncle's nephew. Everyone felt that Eggers was a sort of Charlie McCarthy, sitting on his uncle's lap. Two years later, Eggers and his commissioners came up for election. Brethren, what an election that was!

To understand it I must point out that John V. Kenny, leader of the second ward, was a parishioner at St. Michael's. He is a small, quiet man with a fine smile, a man who would rather be off-stage than on. He worked hard for Hague for thirty years, and the rewards were meager. Still, he did not complain. However, shortly after Eggers became mayor, the Hague forces charged Kenny with trying to ease a relative into a good job at the county jail. Now, Hague had an implacable credo which worked well for many years: the moment one of my boys begins to show his head above the rest of the crowd, shoot him. And that's what they did to John V. Kenny. They read him out of the Democratic party and said that, in the future, another man would be recognized as political leader of the Horseshoe.

The die was cast. Kenny was forced either to fight his old friend to the death or to step down into oblivion. Kenny elected to fight. It was one of the few tactical errors made by Hague. He threw Kenny out at a time when the people were confused about his own administration. The loyalty they felt was to him, not to his nephew. Another large group felt that Hague was through—that he had enjoyed over a quarter of a century of unlimited power, and therefore it was time to give someone else a chance. Perhaps most imporant, thousands of voters downtown were outraged because they knew of the times that Kenny, secretly, had sent the rent money, or a ton of coal, or clothing for the kids. These latter became the most vociferous campaigners for Kenny in all other parts of the city. Lastly, automatic voting machines had been installed, and it was now impossible for Hague's henchmen to tell how a citizen voted.

The election occurred in May of 1949. Throughout the campaign a feeling of tension and fear pervaded the city. Friendships were broken up over a loosely expressed political opinion. The Hague spies reported every word they heard to City Hall, and whole families were lopped off the public payroll. Deputy Mayor Malone carried on an old-fashioned campaign of vituperation, denouncing Kenny and predicting dire things for all who opposed Eggers.

I stuck to the gospel. I made no public utterance on the subject. After all, Frank Hague had been a St. Michael's boy, and Frank Eggers and John Kenny grew up in the parish. Privately, I was sympathetic to Kenny, because I knew him as a person of sterling character, but mostly, I think, because the blows rained upon his head were foul and unfair. I too believed that Hague had served his purpose and his time, and that now was the hour to start afresh, with new faces. I have never shirked a fight in my life, and it irritated me to have to stand on the side lines throughout this one.

In the last days of the campaign, it looked as though Kenny didn't stand a chance. The big machine was running over him like a steam roller. Twice during this time I appeared publicly with Kenny and was photographed with him. Still, both of those occasions occurred in the line of duty. The first was at the annual St. Patrick's Day Dinner. I was chaplain of the Sons and Daughters of St. Patrick, and, politics or no politics, I'd be there. John Kenny was a charter mem-

238

ber of the organization, so he had a right to be there. The second occasion was the annual parish benefit for the St. Vincent de Paul Society. Kenny had sponsored this event for twenty years and, as the father of it, was entitled to be present. As pastor of St. Michael's, it would look bad if I *didn't* show up.

And so, the word got around to City Hall that Father McWilliams was in Kenny's corner. This, in the face of orders from City Hall that anyone seen in Kenny's presence, or anyone who might be inclined to grant Kenny the status of a human being, would be politically excommunicated at once. And Hague himself is reported to have said, "We'll not only defeat Kenny, but we'll drive him out of the city."

Still, at the last moment, the two things which told me that Kenny really stood a great chance occurred in direct sequence. Kenny staged a labor rally at Journal Square, and when I saw the thousands and thousands of marchers—and these were only the people who were unafraid—I felt that the tide had turned. The second event was when Hague decided to come home to the Horseshoe for a gigantic rally. He staged this one in P.S. 37, a block away from St. Michael's. As usual, he did it in the large manner. Every able-bodied Democrat from every ward in the city converged on the Horseshoe in marching formation. Brass bands tooted, and the aerial bombs zoomed up into the warm night sky. Policemen on foot and policemen on motorcycles and on horseback kept the crowds back. This was Hague's boyhood home; this was the master returning to his kin.

When he stepped forward on the stand and held up his hand for quiet, the booing started and swept through the crowd, and the Honorable Frank Hague was almost blown off his own reviewing stand. Then I knew. Then I knew for sure. And I have a suspicion that Hague knew too.

239

Kenny won, with a coalition of Democrats and Republicans, 81,074 votes to 59,128. It wasn't even close. The boss was politically dead, killed by the Little David whom he had dismissed with contempt.

I felt highly honored when "Johnny" gave me the first invitation to the inauguration and asked me to give the invocation. City Hall was jammed to the doors and halfway across Grove Street on that fine morning. I had to use my old tactics of line bucking to get through the mob and into the assembly chamber. My feeling was that this was a time to say a little bit more than just a prayer; so, as the flashlights popped and the cameras ground, I said:

"We are here today because the votes of 81,000 people in Jersey City made such an inauguration possible. A simple man in the street said to me the day before election, 'We can't miss, Father, because it's in the hearts of the people.'

"The little man, the simple folk, were tired of being pushed around, haunted with fear and taunted with every type of threat and reprisal. It wasn't the American way of life and, in a popular uprising, they went to the polls and expressed their indignation. It was their way of saying that the day was past when you can put the whole community in a strait jacket and get away with it. Jersey City has once again joined the society of free cities of the United States. Freedom from fear is really an accomplished fact.

"It has been said that some people believe in law and order if they make the laws and execute the orders. Under a dictator such a proposition would be intolerable. In other circumstances, however, such a statement could be a force for good if what we understand by law is an ordinance of reason and justice, promulgated by legitimate authority for the good of all the people. God is the Supreme Governor and Ruler of the universe, and to men legitimately elected to

240

office he communicates a share in that authority. Such men have a grave responsibility and must one day give an account of their stewardship to Him.

"There is a tendency among men in public life today to forget these simple elementary truths and to use public office, not for the common good but for personal gain. The Ten Commandments are wrapped up in moth balls and stored away in the closet of forgotten things. They substitute a code of "ethics" that is at variance with the Decalogue and the Sermon on the Mount. But integrity should be an essential part of public as well as private life. Morality in politics is something devoutly to be wished for.

"My fellow commissioners, this is a great day for you. The eyes of Jersey City are upon you. You have been elected to high office after one of the greatest political battles of the century. I extend to you my heartiest congratulations and remind you that 'Unless God builds the house, in vain do they labor who build it.'

"I know I will be pardoned if I reserve a special word of praise for your new mayor, the Honorable John V. Kenny. We have been friends for more than thirty years, and during that time he has revealed himself as an humble and good parishioner, a great benefactor of St. Michael's Church, a shining character with those rich hues of personality by which the people recognize their favorites. I have seen those qualities develop and mature, reaching their full power and final climax in the recent magnificent campaign he headed with such resounding success.

"And finally, I want to tell you that he began his new career today where all great works should begin—before God at the foot of the altar. Both Mrs. Kenny—his good wife—and himself were present this morning at a special Mass in St. Michael's Convent Chapel. And so, as you have begun

John, may you continue. The best of everything to you and your colleagues.

"May the blessing of God Almighty, the Father, the Son, and the Holy Ghost, descend upon you and remain with you always."

It was, as some said later, quite a mouthful. But it was uttered after the elections were done, and I had so much Irish fight left in me that it had to be said. It couldn't influence any votes, and it made me feel better to be able to say what I thought out loud.

The following September I met William Flanagan, the newly appointed deputy mayor. Now, Bill is a young fellow for such an important job—he succeeded John Malone, Hague's strong right hand—but he is a tall, thin, amiable young man of around thirty, and he manages to take problems in stride. He had been a truck driver, had seen honorable service in the war, and after the war got a job as a reporter on the Jersey *Journal*. He felt so strongly about Kenny that he was rooting for his fellow parishioner before the battlers got into the political ring. Kenny became interested and sent for Flanagan. From that moment on, Kenny's public relations began to improve. In fact, Flanagan did such a handsome job for Kenny that the new mayor asked him to be deputy mayor.

Well, in September I met him and we had a chat. He said, "You don't know it, Father, but His Honor has sent your name to the chancery office for approval by the Archbishop as the new fire chaplain."

I said, "That was nice of the mayor to think of me, but speaking frankly, I had never given the matter a thought."

A little later on, when asked by my superiors if I had sought the position, I answered with a respectful but categorical "no." In due time, I was confirmed for the post by

His Excellency and was sworn in by the new city clerk, James A. Tumulty, Jr. Jim went to great lengths to make this a special ceremony, and some important people were invited to attend. A wire recording was made of the swearing in and of all the speeches. A battery of photographers took pictures of me, and later on the Firemen's Mutual Benevolent Association presented to me the fireman's white helmet, rubber coat, and boots. I felt proud, but in a way I would rather that it had happened to poor Father Corcoran. How he loved the fire engines, the bells and sirens, the excitement.

Some men use a chaplain's job as a sinecure. I wanted to work at it and do whatever I could for the firemen. So I called on big Eugene Ertle, the chief, and we visited and inspected every one of the twenty-three firehouses in the city. In each house I was introduced to the men, and in each one I explained that I wanted to be of help, and at any time that they had problems where I might be of assistance, to please call on me. Well, they didn't wait long. A few days later, a fireman phoned me at the rectory wanting to know if I could get him a couple of tickets for the World Series.

Too many dinners can kill a man, and I have no idea how many I attended in that first year, but there were more than enough. For seventeen years prior to the advent of Kenny, no firemen had been promoted to captain; so, in the first year of the new administration, many were promoted, and each was tendered a dinner in his own firehouse. Naturally, as fire chaplain, I was expected to attend. And I did. I missed not a one, and I can tell you, with authority, that not all the good chefs are in the Waldorf-Astoria.

One of the first things I did was to revive the annual Fire Department Communion breakfast, and I instituted a memorial Mass on Armistice Day for all deceased firemen. In addition to this, I call on every sick fireman, and I attend the services of every fireman who passes away. I give my counsel in personal problems which are presented to me, and I respond to all second- and third-alarm fires and stand by to administer the sacraments or give any other aid I can. Later, I was invited to be chaplain for the Association of Exempt Firemen, and now, in addition to all the other duties, I attend their meetings and go to the house or funeral parlor and conduct services for their dead.

Only once was I called on to go into a burning building where tenants had been trapped on the top floor. It was a bitter-cold morning at seven o'clock, and with helmet, rubber coat, and boots, I splashed through pools of water and up a burned, rickety staircase to the top. The house was still burning, and in a room I found a Negro lady and several children. I did what I could, but they were all dead. I stayed there for quite a while with the firemen, and I was surprised to find that the smoke and hissing steam had little effect on me. I now began to feel like a real fireman!

To serve his Master, St. Francis Xavier, the apostle to Indies and the Far East, became all things to all men. At Christmastime, 1951, another and new opportunity to serve the needy in Christ was urged upon me by prominent citizens who importuned me to accept the presidency of the Jersey City Community Chest. Mindful of the responsibility and aware of the high civic honor implicit in such a selection, I wondered at the propriety of a priest serving as president of this fund-raising federation of a variety of charitable and private social agencies, each operated by Jewish or Christian bodies of diverse faiths. With this valid thought came the subtle temptation to avoid service by rationalizing that I was already doing my bit. This suggestion of the Old Adversary was routed because I realized that the local Chest drives for funds have the support of many of the bishops throughout the nation including the positive endorsement and approval of my own archbishop. Here would further be served the poor of the gospels, the sick, the crippled, the blind, the troubled and lonely—served in His Name through the twentieth-century techniques of fund raising. Here too would the America of tomorrow be aided by the development of youth into God-fearing and substantial citizens. I dared not in conscience reject this opportunity of further service. So I accepted my appointment as president of the Jersey City Community Fund. I have since been told that this was the first appointment of a priest as president of any Community Chest.

In spite of all of these activities, the most important thing for me to remember is that I am, once and forever, a priest. No outside work, no honors, no friendship in high places, can alter that fact. The biggest goal I set for myself in life was to become a priest. Unlike most men with great ambitions, I achieved mine early in life, thirty-five years ago.

The only other ambition that I set for myself was to be a priestly priest, a true man of God. To achieve this it is necessary for the priest to "walk like Christ, talk like Christ, act like Christ, live like Christ, and be like Christ." No mortal person can achieve those goals because Christ was God, but the priest, the good priest, never stops striving toward those goals. Still, Jesus lives through His priesthood, and the priest must prove it through every hour of every day of his life.

Now, you can see that the average priest lives a complex, and enervating, emotional life. He must act like God, but he isn't God. He must sit on his own human emotions, and keep the lid locked tight, because he might express an opinion that isn't Christlike. And often, he fails through his own frailty. After a while he might tend to relax a little, and when he relaxes, his life is apt to become mechanical and to lose its true direction.

And so, in her wisdom, the Catholic Church requires every priest to make a retreat once a year. This is a time of rest, thought, and prayer. Over the period of a year, the flames of idealism are apt to die down, and it is necessary to throw another log on the fire and make it burn brightly again.

Time will tarnish the hardest metal, and it can tarnish a heart too. Slowly, inexorably, we get away from serving God in the manner we should. There is a need to rededicate ourselves to Him—our bodies with all their senses, our souls with all their faculties, our hearts with all their affections. We have given all to God and should take nothing back. We should love, yes, but only as it serves to bring us closer to Him.

It is at this time of retreat that the priest gets the answer to "How am I doing?" and he gets it right between the two eyes. With no punches pulled and in no uncertain terms he finds out how he has succeeded or failed in his work. When the portrait of the God-man he represents is unveiled before him, he hangs his head in shame as he realizes how far short he has fallen. The shabby reflection he sees of himself in the mirror of Christ's perfection causes him to moan, "Oh, God, be merciful to me, a sinner. . . . Good Master, what shall I do, that I may receive life everlasting?"

The basis of all the retreats I have ever made were the Spiritual Exercises of St. Ignatius, the founder of the Society of Jesus. The retreat master was usually a Jesuit, and under his skillful direction we were brought back to the zeal, the piety, and the devotion we had when we first came from the hands of the ordaining prelate.

Through a series of conferences and meditations we were exhorted to know Christ better, love Him more ardently,

246

and follow Him more closely. The whole course was laid out in a design to (1) cleanse the soul, (2) rebuild its structure in the pattern of the Divine Model, and (3) call forth a rededication of ourselves to the Son of God. We were asked, "What have I done for Christ?" and, in reply, would jot down our chief sins and weaknesses. Then, "What am I doing for Christ?"—the replies to which were to remind us of what we must avoid and what we must do concerning our work and our spiritual life. And finally, "What ought I do for Christ?"—the answer to which was the means we must use to put our resolutions into practice and renew our old-time fervor.

The importance of prayer and morning meditation, plus a spiritual examination at night, were always the high spots in every retreat and they had to be if, as the retreat master said, we are to have a clergy that will walk worthy of the vocation to which it has been called. A Trappist Father from the Abbey of Our Lady of Gethsemane wrote a pamphlet for priests a decade ago. It was called "The God-man's Double," and it brought out the same thought, quite eloquently.

"How can we ever double," he wrote, "without an intimate knowledge of the Original? A real artist never paints from memory; he has his model ever before him. A real sculptor works with hammer and chisel, but his eye is ceaselessly traveling to his model. And any priest who thinks he can be a real priest without always keeping his eye on Christ —is attempting the absurd and essaying the utterly impossible."

His suggestion was to look at the Model every morning for twenty or thirty minutes and then at night to look at the man who is trying to reproduce that Model. Such procedure will reveal to the priest when he fails, where he fails, why he fails. As one priest I can say to that Trappist, "You are so right. It is an unfailing recipe for personal sanctity and great holiness in life."

Throughout the retreat many temporary altars are furnished for all the priests to celebrate daily Mass, and many outside confessors are called in for the retreat confessions. No pains are spared to make this event the most complete spiritual inventory that can be taken.

From the retreat the priest returns to his church washed and refreshed, renewed and lighthearted, happy to be back among his flock, eager to help them. Despair and exhaustion are far away, now. The priest is determined that, in this ensuing year, he is going to be closer to the image and the likeness of God than ever before. It's a spiritual uplift, a supernatural tonic which revitalizes all our activities for Christ.

It is quite possible to conceive, and altogether probable, that before the coming of Christ the Holy Trinity held a conference to determine what to do with this world that man had spoiled. It was a godless world then, just as this one is a Christless world.

God's holiness precluded His doing anything about it; God's justice had discharged all claims that could be made against it. But God's mercy said, "I will go down and become one of them." And so the plan of God's incarnation and redemption were conceived. He left the happiness of heaven for the troubles of earth. Behind all this was but one purpose—to bring man back to God.

We know how He worked. There was Mary Magdalen at the feast in Simon's house about whom He said, "Many sins are forgiven her because she has loved much—thy faith hath made thee safe; go in peace." And the woman taken in adultery: "Woman, where are they that accuse thee? Hath no man condemned thee?" She said, "No man, Lord," and

Jesus said, "Neither will I condemn thee. Go now and sin no more." It is a never-ending story of compassion and the bringing of joy to troubled hearts.

The great powers He has given to me, and to all His other priests, is for the sole purpose of keeping Christ alive in the world—His mercy, His goodness, His forgiveness. In a word, all that Christ was to His time on earth, all priests are charged with being in this day and age. We must strive, harder and harder, to re-create Him among the people with whom we work.

I am still amazed by many things. I am neither a great churchman nor a great man. I am small and weak and erring in both fields. If I can be given a creditable mark for anything, it is for trying. With the tenacity of my forebears, I never give up. I marvel at the mystery of my vocation; I am amazed still at my ordination, now in its thirty-fifth year; I am humbled and somewhat stunned at my elevation in the priesthood.

And yet, in many ways, I am a failure. How many times have I said to myself, "Oh, dear God, give me the chance to start as Thy servant once more!" I kneel in Church before the Blessed Sacrament or sit in my room, and I spend the long hours in solitude, praying, thinking, praying. The bones are getting older. They creak on the stairs and in unison with the stairs. The mind takes a little longer to decide weighty problems. It is slower than it once was, more deliberate, if I may frame an alibi.

I have seen so much, so very, very much. And practically all that I've seen has been in one church, St. Michael's. I have seen great friends come and go with the ticktock of the clock. They were kindly people, good people to a young and frightened curate. But now many of them are gone, and now, as pastor, I peer through my glasses at newer, younger people. My generation is being replaced, even though I'm not yet sixty years of age. There are new young fathers in the Holy Name Society; big fellows who saw service in the war. They look like kids to me, but tomorrow they will be taking the lead in the city and the county and the country.

The earth moves slowly eastward. And on it images of God are born and grow up and make their mark or miss it, and die, to be buried beneath its crust. Then the judgment. And now, in these later years, for me God's peopled sphere seems to be turning faster and ever faster. It is morning, and I have so many things to do. Before half of them are done it is morning again, and there are new tasks. My younger curates tell me to take matters easy. How familiar that sounds! It seems only the day before yesterday that I was telling pastors to take it easy. I stand in the downstairs hall and watch their lithe, supple bodies bounce up the stairs two at a time, and I remember—and how I remember!—when I used to do that.

Time moves inexorably for all of us. You cannot slow it down, nor can you speed it up. And someday, for each of us, time will cease to be. There is a given moment when it will stop for all eternity. When it stops for me, I hope that I can attain what St. Paul said in his second epistle to Timothy:

"Carefully study to present thyself approved unto God, a workman that needeth not to be ashamed, rightly handling the word of truth."

I want to be a workman unashamed.

Date Due